The Times Reports
The French Revolution

The Times Reports

The French Revolution

Extracts from *The Times* 1789–1794

**Introduced and edited by
Neal Ascherson**

Preface by Colin Bell
Series Editor

TIMES BOOKS

First published in Great Britain in 1975 by Times Books, the book
publishing division of Times Newspapers Limited, New Printing
House Square, London WC1X 8EZ

ISBN   0 7230 0129 4 (cased)
ISBN   0 7230 0132 4 (paper)

Designed by John Lucioni

Copies of original material from The Times
contained in this book were supplied by
Newspaper Archive Developments Limited, Reading

Printed in Great Britain by
Tinling (1973) Ltd, Prescot, Merseyside
(a member of the Oxley Printing Group Ltd.)

CONTENTS

PREFACE

The Times is perhaps the best-known newspaper in the world, and only 'perhaps' because one must allow for those great nations which no longer permit their citizens to know of any newspapers but their own. It is not the oldest — not yet quite 200 years old — nor the thickest, the richest or, at least beyond all argument, the best; but it is, and has been for the greater part of its history, among the best, and among the most influential. Foreign governments have frequently suspected that it spoke for the British government; British governments, that it spoke for the most important section of the British people. It is an institution, to be ranked in the social history of Britain alongside the Civil Service, the Church and the Monarchy, rather than among the rest of the Press.

This unique standing gives a special status to its files. They contain, of course, the news stories of the past, and those stories were rarely covered more extensively in any other paper, although on occasion more perceptively. But the full significance of *The Times*'s coverage of any great event is not that it is a newspaper of record, supplying the historian and the student with contemporary raw material; it is that *The Times* is itself an important actor in the drama.

Sometimes this importance lay, as we have seen, in the tendency of foreigners to take *The Times*'s views as official, and there have certainly been periods when Westminster and White-hall helped shape what was said in Printing House Square. Whether this was the result of straight corruption, as with Pitt's subsidy to the paper in the 1790s, or natural identity of view, as with the close consultations Dawson had with Baldwin or Halifax in the 1930s, it must be said that there have been times when those foreigners have been right. Sometimes, too, the view of *The Times* has reflected what the British Government might want to do, or want to be thought to want. There is no better place for any politician to float a 'trial balloon', and however scrupulously a newspaper resists such attempts, it cannot always tell in time that this is what is happening. So to look at history through *The Times* is on occasion to see what other countries believed, or were led to believe, was Britain's policy.

This very authority, this dominating position among the

Press, has meant that British governments have been just as sensitive themselves to what *The Times* has said, since others might think that some particular stand represented Whitehall's orders to *The Times*. Whitehall has always been aware that it might as easily represent middle-class England's orders to Whitehall. The paper rapidly established, in the era of Barnes and of Delane, a solid command of circulation among the civil servants, academics, leading industrialists and financiers, among the Justices of the Peace and Lords Lieutenant, country parsons and army officers, among that class which constituted for so long 'political England'. It was the newspaper in which they told each other of their births, marriages and deaths, in which they advertised their needs and wants — frequently bizarre — and in which they addressed themselves to their peers on any subject which seemed to them important. They drew their information about the world from *The Times*; and when they had any views about the world, they sent a letter to the Editor. Politicians know all about 'constituency opinion', and they know therefore that a newspaper too has got its own constituency; in the case of *The Times*, a very powerful one, whose opinions matter. So to look at history through *The Times* can also be to see what political England believed, or what the British government thought that they believed.

Not all leaders in *The Times* echoed Whitehall, or the readers' known or suspected views; most probably the majority of those which evoked that special tone which has led to the paper's nickname of 'The Thunderer', sprang from the Editor and his little group of leader-writers, informed and advised by the paper's specialist reporters and correspondents. Arguably because it has so often spoken for other powers in the State, *The Times* has long been a power in its own right, a leader of opinion as well as the channel for opinions. What is printed about a dynamic situation becomes itself part of that situation; if *The Times* takes a line hitherto ignored, then it can be ignored no longer. Rejected, opposed, amended, but not ignored, so that it is frequently impossible to look at history without *The Times*.

All these points made with particular reference to the leaders and the letters, can equally be applied to the news reports. A report in *The Times* may, and very often does, tell posterity what actually happened; but even when posterity has discovered that *The Times* got it wrong, it remains true that what was reported was what was necessarily believed at the time to be the case. Believed not only by the English educated public, but by Government, whose own sources of information were by no means always as good as, let alone better than, those of the paper, and believed by much of the rest of the world. Once more, if what the paper said was not in fact right, but was the information on which a decision was taken, a political stance adopted, it is of historical significance. It may not clinch many arguments to say 'but I read it in the papers', but in the absence of compelling proof, to cite *The Times* carries special weight.

That weight derives, quite properly, from the reputation of the paper's staff, and from the unimpeachable accuracy of much of what it carries. In this series matter easily obtainable elsewhere, such as Parliamentary Debates, Law Reports, texts of Treaties, major speeches, White Papers and Royal Commission Reports, has had to be excluded, but the fact that *The Times* carries such material, recognises the responsibilities of a newspaper of record, necessarily reflects not only on the reader's acceptance of what else he reads, but on the reporter's and sub-editor's approach to every other story. *Times* men may be misled, misinformed, may make mistakes of judgement, but with rare exceptions they can be assumed to be reporting rather than propagandising or entertaining. Their copy may prove of propaganda use, and may indeed be entertaining, but the first consideration, *The Times* angle, is usually to relay what happened.

This series has been conceived, then, with two aims in mind: the first is to give the general reader a view of great historical events as they were seen at the time by a great newspaper, a view which is often just as accurate as, and far more vigorous and enthralling than, that offered by a modern textbook. The second aim is to give the more serious student, and the specialist, a time-saving tool, which, although it cannot free him entirely from the labour of ploughing through bound volumes or microfilm in search of his subject, makes *The Times* as accessible as it is indispensable.

On every subject there has had to be extensive editing. Important topics have usually been recognised as such at the time, and *The Times* covers important topics thoroughly. Every editor in this series makes his first priority the telling of the story — using the news reports to make clear the development of events. Thereafter, he chooses leaders which show what the state of opinion was, or which are now known to have carried great influence, letters which illustrate public reaction, or which had repercussions of significance, news stories, right or wrong, which demonstrate what was then thought to be happening, and 'unmissables': the unmissables are those items which are too good to miss — the report of a minor battle by Russell, a letter from Keynes with the first glimmerings of Keynesianism, a speech by the young Churchill which takes the modern reader by surprise, a leader which proclaims the imminent victory of the Confederacy.

The editors themselves are drawn from scholarship and from journalism, not separately and distinctly, but from those with experience of both, since this series is about history, but history as seen by, and influenced by, a newspaper. It is of some importance whether a particular story is carried across the main news page, or relegated to the bottom of a column on some remote page near the classified advertisements, and of importance, too, to know what the effect of deadlines can be on the accuracy of a story.

The notes which the editors have contributed are designed to make such points, as well as to supply such information as non-specialists may need, and which the original readers knew already, and to put each excerpt in its context. Unless specifically marked, they have made no cuts *within* any excerpt, nor any alterations, save to typographical errors and, occasionally, punctuation.

COLIN BELL

INTRODUCTION

In 1785, there appeared in London a paper called the *Daily Universal Register*. It did not attract much attention. At the beginning of 1788, the title changed to *The Times*. But the paper remained a feeble, sensationalizing sheet, and other London dailies, like the *Morning Chronicle*, had a more solid reputation.

A year later there began in Paris a quarter-century of revolution and war which was the making of *The Times*, since it contrived to cling to this huge trellis of events while sending down permanent roots. The *Morning Chronicle* was supreme on home politics: *The Times* went for foreign news and war reporting. By the time of Waterloo the paper's stiffest opponents conceded *The Times* respect for its twenty-five years of coverage of French affairs.

No historian today would use that coverage as his principal source. *The Times* got many things wrong. Obstructive winds in the Channel delayed despatches from Paris, or brought them in the wrong order. Censorship set in. Haste by correspondents or translators sometimes produced texts of revolutionary documents wildly at variance with the originals now available. Prejudice and bungling played their own part: *The Times* missed the Tennis Court Oath, and dismissed news of the French victory at Valmy — Goethe's 'new age in the history of the world' — as propaganda. This coverage, however, though inaccurate, is of primary importance in illustrating what England knew, or thought she knew, of France.

And yet the sheer scale of this coverage remains astonishing. *The Times* was a single sheet of paper, folded once to give four pages. It frequently gave a third of this space or more, advertising included, to reports from France. Most debates in the National Assembly, Legislative Assembly and Convention, and some in the Jacobin Club, were carried in long verbatim extracts. That queer old column starting with Court news and ending in anecdotes about the bed-hopping of the ruling class — the stock from which the news pages eventually branched — always included paragraphs about events in France.

All this cost a great deal of money. Paris correspondents had to be paid; so did the gentlemen hired to translate the French, Dutch and German press in the London office at Printing House

Square. There were subscriptions to these foreign papers, and large sums payable to release them from Customs. Communications were horribly costly (10d. — perhaps £1 in modern currency — for a letter from France or Flanders); the proprietor at one time engaged some Kent smugglers to get his mail across the Channel more efficiently than the Calais and Dieppe packets. And this was a bad period for newspaper finances. Circulation rose fast during the Revolution, but even in 1792 *The Times* was only selling some 2,900 copies. The papers were then mostly read in the coffee-houses, where they passed through many hands. Subscriptions were rare. Again the yield from the relatively high cover price, rising from 4d to 4½d, was offset by the deliberately sharp taxes levied on each copy of the paper (stamp tax) and upon advertising. In the last decades of the century, it was almost impossible to keep a daily paper profitable through conventional sources of income.

The result was easy to predict. *The Times*, like all the London press of the day, had to find a rich patron who would pay a newspaper to back him and his views. Occasionally *The Times* sank to exploiting 'suppression money' in exchange for its promise not to print discreditable anecdotes. But the main source of backstairs income, political subsidy, was regarded as fairly respectable. A political group, in government or opposition, would pay for support, sometimes through an annuity to the 'Conductor' of a newspaper. In return, the paper was expected to print news items, commentaries and even fragments of slanderous gossip sent down to the office, sometimes composed by junior members of an administration. A further and most formidable inducement to loyalty was the granting of first access to foreign despatches and intelligence which arrived through official channels. Misbehaviour could lose a newspaper this privilege. Elements of this eighteenth-century technique of press management survive to this day in Britain in the form of the 'lobby system' — access to official background information which can, if abused, be denied.

In the years of the Revolution and the wars which ensued, *The Times* was under the wing of the Pitt administration. The paper was originally founded by Walter, a failed underwriter, as a way of publicizing his new 'logographic' printing system (one of those bright ideas which make the compositor's life more difficult rather than less). Walter made a play for the favour of the younger Pitt by supporting him in his struggle to keep the Prince of Wales and his supporter Fox out of power during the madness of George III. He was rewarded early in 1789 by the grant of a £300 allowance, which continued until his son William offended the ruling ministry ten years later. 'Happening to be at the Treasury at the beginning of last year,' John Walter wrote in 1790, 'Mr Steele called Me into his Room, & after paying Me some Compliments on the Stability of my Conduct, at a Time when other Papers were veering round to the rising Sun,[1] made Me an offer of £300 a year, to support the Measures of Government, which I acquiesced in . . .'

Following Pitt turned out to be a rough ride. Walter's patrons sent him some paragraphs suggesting that the Duke of York and the Prince were appalled when the King temporarily regained his sanity. Both sued, and John Walter was sentenced to a £50 fine, two hours in the pillory (which was remitted) and a total of sixteen months in prison. He loyally refused to betray the origin of the paragraphs. In June 1791, following his release after 14 miserable months in Newgate, he was rewarded with £250 out of Secret Service funds.

Another crisis blew up in 1792. Pitt's press managers, Evan Nepean and Henry Dundas, began to pass official despatches to Walter's rivals, the *Sun* and the *True Briton*. Walter's son William wrote to Dundas in September 1793 complaining that 'scarce a Dispatch comes from the Armies, or is there a Paris Journal forwarded to any of the Public Offices, but what is immediately transmitted to the *Sun* office . . .'

The background may have been the government's alarm about the spread of revolutionary literature in Britain, which raised press management to the status of an operation in defence of the whole social order. Nepean and Dundas believed that Chauvelin, the French ambassador, was paying several London papers to present 'seditious' doctrines, and probably decided to cast their own net more widely. They had no possible cause for complaint against *The Times*, which by 1792 was attacking the Revolution and its British supporters with hysterical violence. William's letter took effect, and Dundas later dropped his experiment with the *Sun*.

Does it make sense, then, to look for an authentic '*Times*

---

[1] i.e. the Prince of Wales.

view' of the Revolution, if so much of its contents was paid puff? I think it does. Journalists graft easily into the trunk of their patrons' opinions: the *Times* men rapidly made themselves at home in the developing views of Pitt and his friends.

The States-General, the first French parliament to be summoned since 1614, opened its session on May 5th, 1789. *The Times* found this a tremendous and happy event. Like most British observers, the paper saw the first phase of the Revolution in the light of recent British history, and supposed that 1789 would prove a French 1688, bringing to France the benefits of constitutional and limited monarchy and introducing internal free trade. But, as the extracts show, *The Times* was soon disconcerted to find that the Third Estate, the Commons, was claiming for itself the right to represent the whole nation, a demand which did not fit with the pattern of the Glorious Revolution at all and instead recalled the behaviour of the Long Parliament. Was there to be no House of Lords? How could there be liberty if one part of society was attempting to over-power another?

Only days before the attack on the Bastille, *The Times* for July 9th was obviously worried about the extremism and 'violence' of Third Estate oratory. 'It is much to be feared that the troubles have only yet a beginning', the paper commented on the 14th itself, unaware of how strenuously Paris was fulfilling this prophecy the same day. No revolution could be 'glorious' if it led to 'trouble', by which *The Times* meant a popular movement on the streets and out of the control of authority. In the following weeks, the Paris crowd began to destroy the 1688 parallel by spontaneous armed action, and by bringing rank and even monarchy itself into question.

By the end of the year, after the Parisians had marched to Versailles in October and brought the royal family back to the capital, the temperature in the streets was dropping again and the National Assembly was embarking on its year of radical reforms. *The Times*, as the extracts show, was often confused about how to take these events. In general, the further the Revolution developed away from the British paradigm, the less the paper liked it. This was not a matter of thought-out ideology. *The Times* adopted neither the doctrines of the Rights of Man and popular sovereignty, nor, at the other extreme, the organic conservatism of Burke, which seemed to sacrifice the individual's rights to a higher collectivism. At Printing House Square, they stuck to less lofty themes. The abolition of titles of nobility, in June 1790, was condemned: 'distinctions . . . are the right of society'. On the other hand, the journalism over these two years was inconsistent, veering between satisfaction that a 'despotic' monarchy was getting what it deserved, and outrage at physical threats to the sacred persons of a King and Queen. By the end of 1790 *The Times* was beginning to share Pitt's own doubts that France would ever 'unite the liberty she had acquired with the blessings of law and order'.

As late as March 1791, however, the émigré forces gathering against France were still 'the army of malcontents', and the paper seems to have hoped that a chastened King could ally himself with loyal moderates of the Revolution to defeat the twin extremes of emigration and the Jacobin Club (now preaching 'a rank Republic'). But after the flight of the royal family to Varennes in June and their virtual arrest, *The Times* promoted the 'malcontents' to the 'Counter Revolution'. From then on, *The Times* treated revolutionary France with almost total hostility.

In 1792, the Revolution and the kingdoms of Europe went to war. Within France, the tide of popular insurrection began to run again. It was, of all the Revolutionary years, the year of the Paris crowd. The people swept into the Tuileries in June, rallied to the 'patrie en danger' in July, and carried through the great insurrection of August 10th which ended the 'constitutional' phase and opened the way to revolutionary dictatorship in the name of the people. In the first days of September they turned hysterically upon the 'inner enemy' and butchered the inhabitants of the prisons. *The Times* shuddered. Internal evidence shows that the Paris correspondent at this period was actually a Frenchman (see, for instance, his report of the August 10th insurrection), and evidently a royalist Frenchman at that, who regarded monarchy as more divine than limited. Atrocities were noticed, occasionally even invented, with relish. The detained royal family, 'despots' two years before, now became 'August Personages'.

At the end of the year the King went on trial, and on January 21st, 1793, two days after the Convention had condemned him to death by a narrow majority, he was guillotined. *The Times* helped Pitt to prepare the country for war: 'armed with fire and sword, we must penetrate into the recesses of this land of blood and carnage'. A casual reader must have supposed that Britain was launching a conservative crusade to suppress the Revolution. Evidently, *The Times* preferred to see matters so, for the real sequence of events — it was France which declared war, in order to forestall British resistance to the intended invasion of Holland — was not much emphasized.

But in the course of 1793, a surprising change stole over the paper's French coverage. In spite of the war, in spite of the Terror, the tone of moral outrage flagged. Instead, Printing House Square began to produce an equivalent of modern 'Kremlinology', well-informed columns discussing the political battles within the Convention and the power base of each group and personality. Patterns of revolutionary politics were identified ('the minority had constantly effected the destruction of the majority'), which enabled *The Times* to make some successful predictions, especially after the moderate 'Girondins' were overthrown by the second popular insurrection of May 31st, 1793. Robespierre's dictatorship and the 'revolutionary government' of December, the fall of the Hébertists and the Dantonists in early 1794, led to a decline in Robespierre's support which *The Times* was able to analyse. On July 28th, 1794 (10 Thermidor), Robespierre himself was finally brought down.

The anonymity of *The Times*'s correspondents, who put down such vivid and opinionated impressions of Paris, is not yet penetrable. The papers of John Walter I tell us nothing. *The Times* itself shows only that several 'Gentlemen' were sent from London at various times, and that a 'regular Correspondent' — the French royalist — was operating during 1792. Private letters, many probably from members of the British Embassy, supplemented their work. But it was the correspondents who took the risks and pains, and it is they who must take the principal honour for the material in this book.

NEAL ASCHERSON

CHRONOLOGY OF THE FRENCH REVOLUTION

1789

May 5	Opening of States-General, Versailles.
June 20	Tennis Court Oath.
July 14	Fall of the Bastille.
October 5	March to Versailles.

1790

June 19	Abolition of Nobility.
July 12	Civil Constitution of the Clergy.
July 14	Fête of Federation (first anniversary).

1791

June 20	Flight to Varennes.
July 11	Voltaire reburied in Panthéon.
July 14	Birmingham Riots.
July 17	Massacre of Champ de Mars.
August 27	Declaration of Pillnitz: Austria and Prussia threaten war.
September 14	Louis XVI accepts new Constitution.
October 1	First meeting of new Legislative Assembly.

1792

March 10	The Brissotin ministry.
April 20	Declaration of war on Austria.
June 13	Brissotin ministry falls.
June 20	Paris crowd breaks into Tuileries.
August 1	Manifesto of Duke of Brunswick.
August 9	Insurrectional Commune of Paris.
August 10	Storm of Tuileries.
August 11	National Convention called.
August 13	Royal Family confined in Temple.
September 2	Fall of Verdun; beginning of 'Septembrisades' — prison massacres.
September 20	Battle of Valmy.
September 21	Abolition of royalty.
November 6	Battle of Jemappes.
December 3	Convention resolves to try Louis.
December 26	Trial opens.

1793

January 18	King condemned to death.
January 21	King's execution.
February 1	War declared on Britain and Holland.
March 7	War declared on Spain.
March 8–10	'March Days'.
March 10	Insurrection in Vendée begins.
April 4	Dumouriez deserts to enemy.
April 6	Committee of Public Safety set up.
April 13	Marat impeached.
June 2	Fall of the 'Girondins'.
June 24	Constitution of 1793.
July 13	Marat murdered by Charlotte Corday.
October 10	Provisional Government decree.
October 16	Execution of Marie-Antoinette.
October 31	Execution of the 'Girondins'.
November 10	Festival of Reason, Notre-Dame.
December 4	Revolutionary Government.

1794

March 23	Execution of Hébert and supporters.
April 5	Execution of Danton and supporters.
May 7	Cult of the Supreme Being.
June 1	'Glorious First of June'.
June 10	'Law of 22 Prairial'.
July 27 (9 Thermidor)	Proscription of Robespierre and followers.
July 28 (10 Thermidor)	Execution of Robespierre.

FRANCE

THE STATES GENERAL

We have already mentioned the meeting of the States General, and shall now continue the subject. The public will perceive the authenticity as well as early communication of our intelligence. A Gentleman at Versailles is engaged by this Paper to transmit us every particular on this important business, who will attend the proceedings regularly whenever the Assembly meets.

On Monday evening, the 4th instant, the King and Heralds at Arms, dressed in their violet coloured robes, richly decorated with the French Arms, and wearing white satin slippers, proclaimed, on horseback, by the sound of the trumpet, the opening of the States General on Tuesday last, at eight o'clock in the morning, at Versailles.

On Tuesday at nine the Deputies were all met. The Heralds then called them over according to the rank of the places they represented; this took up three hours, and at twelve o'clock HIS MAJESTY arrived in his State Coach.

The nearest idea we can give of the brilliancy of this spectacle, is the Court of Justice now sitting at Westminster Hall on Mr. Hastings's Trial. Accommodations were prepared in the Court for all the Ladies of rank and foreigners of distinction, besides other galleries set apart for strangers. The throne was considerably raised, and the Court was not divided with partitions as in the time of Louis the XI, but all the orders of the State mixed together.

The KING's Speech lasted about seven minutes, and was spoken with great eloquence and dignity, but the buzz of the Court did not allow it to be distinctly heard, nor is there an exact copy yet printed. HIS MAJESTY said, that although he knew the extent of his prerogatives, he required no other than that of being the SINCEREST FRIEND OF ALL HIS SUBJECTS. (Here he was interrupted by the loudest and most flattering applause. The QUEEN, who sat a little below the King, joined in it most heartily.) His Majesty then proceeded to state the situation of the kingdom, and declared, that the present annual deficiencies exceeded the revenues 57 millions of livres, or 2,375,000*l.* sterling; that a

1

deficiency had always existed before his coming to the throne, which had been considerably augmented by the late war.

The Keeper of the Seals spoke next, and after him Mr. NECKER. The latter was on his legs half an hour, when finding himself fatigued, he requested that the rest of his speech might be read, which was done by *M. Broussonnet,* Secretary to the Royal Society of Agriculture.

In speaking of the Finances, Mr. NECKER, in like manner with the King, stated, that the deficiency of the annual revenues amounted to 57 millions.[1] This calculation exactly corresponds with that given in by the Minister at the first assembly of the Notables, when the deficiency was computed at 112 millions, without including 55 millions of reimbursements. The Minister next proposed the mode of equalizing the receipt and expenditure, which he said might be accomplished in two years without any further taxes, by the abolition of some particular pensions and places, contributions of the Farmers General, and other public companies. He next required, that the State of the *Caisse d'Escompte* should be laid before the States General. But what should most render this Assembly immortal, was a proposition to abolish the *Corvee,* or an imposition on the lower class of people to keep in repair the public roads at their own expence, to which they must employ a certain portion of their time and cattle. Some modifications were likewise proposed to be adopted in favor of the slaves in the West Indies.

Another principal object of this speech, was the important consideration, in what manner the votes should be taken, whether by the plurality of numbers, or of each order. M. Necker proposed that this question should be speedily determined, and that the three orders should each name deputies to discuss this great preliminary object, — to meet it under every circumstance, and find out some method to unite in sentiment.

Among other things, the Minister declared, that it was the King's earnest desire to see himself surrounded by his people, not only once, but always. That the mode of assessing the rate of taxes, and what each county should pay, should be settled in the Provincial Assemblies, as they must be the best judges of their own riches and resources.

---

[1] The figure given for the British equivalent of the 57 million livres deficit seems to be a misprint. J. M. Thompson, in *The French Revolution* (Blackwell, 1959 edition) quotes an equivalent of £280,000.

M. Necker threw out some few hints concerning the future legislation of the kingdom: they tended to assure a periodical meeting of the States General, the liberty of individuals, and, moreover, the liberty of the press. He, however, asserted the King's exclusive right of the executive power, and that his Majesty would never permit it to be divided from him.

The 'Gentleman' covering the occasion for The Times *was accurate in his descriptions but too optimistic in his account of the mood of the States General. Necker's recipe for adjusting the financial deficit 'without any further taxes' went down badly: if the States General were to have no control of taxation, the main weapon of constitutional government would be denied to parliament. The States General also felt that Necker's remarks about 'what manner the votes should be taken' amounted to stalling, rather than to an assurance that the question would be 'speedily determined'. The Gentleman, in fact, reflected the early hope of* The Times *that the problems of absolutism and economic misery could be solved without weakening the position of royalty.*

On June 17th, the Third Estate constituted itself as the 'National Assembly'. When Louis closed the Parliament House, the deputies met in the royal tennis courts at Versailles on the 20th and, by the 'oath of the jeu de paume', swore to continue their meetings until 'the constitution of the realm is set up and consolidated on firm foundations'. The Times *did not report the 'Tennis Court Oath' but — unlike other French and British observers — was shrewd enough to see that the precarious victory of the Third Estate was not the happy end of the whole struggle. The paper's business information was good, and on the same page as the extract below appeared an account of the latest increase in bread prices, with a forecast of trouble.*

July 3rd, 1789

FRANCE

Late on Wednesday night arrived an express from the Duke of DORSET[1] at Paris.

[1] The Duke of Dorset was the British Ambassador in France.

By the accounts contained in private letters from the same place, we have every reason to believe, that the power of the King of France is verging to a conclusion. The tumult occasioned by the Royal Sittings has produced a very great fermentation among the people. The French Guards at Paris, amounting to 4000 men, have refused to obey the King's orders, and declared themselves to be the SOLDIERS OF THE NATION. The DUC DE CHATELET, their Colonel, went to Versailles and assured the King, that he could not answer for his safety, if he continued to enforce the Royal Orders. On this information, his Majesty wrote to the *Order of Noblesse,* and expressed his wish that they would join the *Third Estate,* and incorporate with them, which they did. The Clergy had already done the same. As the *Third Estate,* with those of the Nobility and Clergy who have joined them, form a majority of 800 against 300, there is no doubt but that every resolution taken in the National Assembly, will be in favour of the Third Estate. In short, it appears as if nothing could prevent the new modelling of the Constitution, according to their pleasure. One of the first steps will be, to annull whatever the King had asserted at the Royal Sitting, that tended to oppose the rights claimed by the Third Estate. The idea entertained by the Army, of the intention of the Third Estate to encrease their pay, has had its effect, and won that powerful body to the cause of liberty.

July 9th, 1789

In the national assembly, the debates continue to be carried on with increasing violence, and bid defiance to monarchy. M. DE MIRABEAU is the leader of the patriotic party. The few following expressions, which he made use of in the assembly of the States General, will tend to shew the unlimited freedom of speech which prevails.

'No person on earth, says he, has the right to say in this assembly I WILL, or I ORDER IT. The plenitude of legislative power rests here, and it would be folly for any Member, or any individual whatever, to protest against the proceedings of a whole nation.'

July 14th, 1789

FRANCE

CIVIL COMMOTIONS

In a REVOLUTION, such as is now agitating in France, it is impossible for the best informed mind to judge, with any accuracy, the issue of the present contest. If the information of this paper appears contradictory one day from another, the blame cannot be imputed to us. We are only the faithful daily record of what passes in France, the politics of which we watch with the most diligent enquiries. From the present prospect of affairs, it is much to be feared that the troubles have only yet a beginning.

The Palace at Versailles is completely surrounded by foreign troops. The army under MARSHALL DE BROGLIO,[1] which we mentioned last week to be ordered from *Loraine, Alsace,* &c. composed almost wholly of the Swiss troops, has shewed an uncommon celerity in obeying that summons. The whole corps was not expected till the 15th, whereas a camp of 35,000 men, accompanied by a very large train of artillery, is already formed, and stationed between Paris and Versailles, as a SECURITY to the KING. His MAJESTY takes good care of the Marshall, and is so anxious to have him at hand, that he is lodged in the Palace of Versailles, in the apartments lately belonging to the present Dauphin.

The MARSHALL DE BROGLIO has entered on his command with great firmness and intrepidity. He had not been long arrived, before his activity was called into action: on an insurrection last week at Versailles, the mob threw large stones at a party of Hussars, who were sent to disperse them. They were on horseback with their swords drawn, and finding themselves resisted, they put up their sabres, and withdrew. On receiving further instructions from MARSHALL BROGLIO, and having been joined by two additional companies, they returned with orders, that if the mob would not disperse, they should ride over them sword in hand. This was done, and one of the leaders taken up and sent to prison. The mob soon rallied afresh, and were proceeding towards the prison, when M. DE BROGLIO sent them word, that if they did not immediately desist, the prisoner should

---

[1] Usually spelt 'de Broglie'.

be produced to them, but hanging at the window of it. This threat had its effect, and the mob dispersed.

The assemblage of an army of 35,000 men near Versailles, the avowed purpose of sending for them to protect the King, added to the peculiar mode of appointing MARSHALL BROGLIO, could not be supposed to remain unnoticed by the violent Patriots in the National Assembly.

Accordingly, we find, that the Sittings of the National Assembly on the 8th instant were uncommonly tumultuous, and dispelled the pleasing hope which had been entertained, that when once the Assembly had regularly met, tranquillity would be restored. This was much increased by the unanimity that prevailed on the appointment of a speaker.

The encampment became on the 8th instant, the subject of debate. The meeting was extremely full, and the rumours which had gone abroad on the subject had prepared men's minds for something important.

M. DE MIRABEAU rose, and in a very florid and eloquent speech of two hours, described the critical situation in which the assembly was placed by the arrival of this army. The station of these troops, says he, is subversive of the liberty of this Assembly, contrary to the true interests of the King, and an infringement on the privileged Orders. The purpose for which they are assembled, is not for the re-establishment of tranquillity in Paris, for one word of kindness and soothing has been already found sufficient for that end; besides, his Majesty must be aware that to provision 35,000 men in this time of famine must only increase the public misfortunes. The King is ill advised by some wicked traitors to the constitution, and it behoves us to seek the best remedy in our power. M. de Mirabeau then moved, *that an address be presented to the King, praying that he would take into consideration his own interest as well as the national liberty, and that under the circumstances of the present famine, he would order the troops back with their train of artillery to those places from whence they came; that should his Majesty be fearful of any disturbances at Paris or Versailles, he might raise companies of armed burghers in those towns, who would be at his orders, and a sufficient protection.*

M. de Mirabeau intermixed this discourse with every species of matter which might enflame the minds of the meeting. He pictured these soldiers as taking possession of all the bridges, and eminences where the people might defend their liberties, and called on his fellow citizens not to submit to the yoke. He then moved, that this motion might be again reported the next day in the assembly.

July 20th, 1789

REBELLION AND CIVIL WAR
IN FRANCE

The disputes which have for some time past convulsed this neighbouring kingdom, have at length been brought to a crisis, which no man could have foreseen or supposed. The relation of what PARIS has been during last week, fills the mind with horror; and although we have all seen and felt the sad effects of an unlicensed populace in our own country, at the time of that dreadful conflagration in London during the riots in 1780,[1] yet even that melancholy event was far short of the general distress which not only is felt in Paris, but in the neighbourhood for many leagues around it.

We have no period in the history of Europe since the time of CHARLES the IX, of France, in 1572, affording so striking an example of a distracted Government, and the bloodshed of a civil war, as that which France now exhibits. No personal safety,—no protection of property, and the lives of the first men in the State in such momentary danger, as to oblige them to fly their country, and seek an asylum in this land of liberty. Such is the picture of Paris at this instant; and rebellion has so widely spread, that no one can judge where it will have an end. All public business is stopped, the whole system and strength of Government annihilated, and even the King and Queen obliged to shut themselves up in the palace of Versailles with a strong guard for their own security. . .

. . .

The public are already in possession of M. NECKER's dismission yesterday se'nnight, which was followed by a total change in the French Cabinet. It does not appear that M. NECKER's removal was in consequence of any ill will which the KING bore him; on the contrary, his Majesty shewed him every mark of respect; and it is even said, advised him to resign. It was, however, this

[1] The London riots referred to were the Gordon Riots, June 2, 1780

change in Administration, which was the immediate consequence of the present violent commotions.

They began on the Monday morning, and have continued
unremittingly ever since. It cannot now be said that the present
violences are the effect of a mere unlicenced mob, but they are
the acts of the public at large. The concurrent voice of the nation
demands a new constitution, nor do we foresee that any power
can resist it.

On Monday the people joined in greater numbers than they
had hitherto done, and seemed determined to be revenged for the
insult which they said was offered to them, by removing Mr.
NECKER. Previous thereto the mob had destroyed several of the
toll-gates belonging to the Government in the vicinity of Paris,
as well as the books belonging to the Excise Officers, by which
very large entries of goods passed without paying the revenue,
and every part of the metropolis exhibited a scene of riot.

The regular troops held for the protection of Paris were
persuaded to join the people; they were encamped in the *Champ
de Mars*, to the number of 5000 men, and marched to the *Hotel
of Invalids*, a building in the out-skirts of the city. The invalids
joined the rest, and brought away all the great guns, and other
ammunition, belonging to the Hospital. With this reinforcement
the people then attacked the Bastile Prison, which they soon
made themselves masters of, and released all the State Prisoners
confined there, among whom was Lord MAZARINE,[1] an Irish
Nobleman, who has been confined for debt near 30 years. The
Prisoners in the other Gaols were freed in like manner, excepting
such as were under sentence of death, whom they hung up within
the Prisons. This seemed to argue a premeditated design, as well
as great caution.

On attacking the Bastile they secured the Governor, the
MARQUIS DE L'AUNEY, and the Commandant of the Garrison,
whom they conducted to the *Place de Greve*, the place of public
execution, where they beheaded them, stuck their heads on tent

---

[1] There were in fact only seven prisoners in the Bastile. Lord 'Mazarine'
(Massereene) was not among them. Clotworthy, Earl of Massereene, had served
many years for debt in another prison, the Châtelet, but had escaped in May
after marrying the Governor's daughter, Mlle Bercier. This ornament of Ulster,
'the most superlative coxcomb that Ireland ever bred', once ordered that the
funeral of his favourite hound should be attended by fifty bitches attired in
white scarves.

poles, and carried them in triumph to the *Palais Royal,* and through the streets of Paris. The MARQUIS DE L'AUNEY was particularly odious to the people, from the nature of his employment, and it is therefore no wonder that he should be singled out amongst the first victims of their resentment.

The *Hotel de Ville,* or Mansion-house, was the place that was next attacked. M. de FLESSIL, the *Prevot de Marchand,* or Lord Mayor, had made himself obnoxious by attempting to read publicly some instructions he had received from the King. In doing this he was stabbed in several places, his head cut off, and carried away, M. de CROSNE, the *Lieutenant de Police,* shared the same fate, only that he was hung up in the public streets.

Several other very violent excesses have been committed. The Duc de LATREMOUILLE, and many other Noblemen the friends of the king, who voted against the *Tiers Etat,* the people have confined in prison. The Duc de LUXEMBOURG, one of the most conspicuous of that order, got away with some difficulty, and arrived in London on Saturday night with all his family. The Duc de CHATELET, Colonel of the King's Guard, very narrowly escaped assassination. He was mounted on horseback, attended by some Hussars, and the people were about to stop him, when some of them called out to let him escape adding, *that though he was a rascal, they would not take away his life.*

The number of armed men in Paris is supposed to amount to 300,000 men, and they call themselves the Militia. The way by which so many people have procured arms is, that all the public store-houses where weapons were lodged, have been broken open, as well as several private houses plundered, which they thought contained them.

The QUEEN and the Count d'ARTOIS are the principal persons of the public detestation. Large rewards have been offered for both, and *placards* or handbills are posted at every avenue of the streets, offering 500,000 livres for the QUEEN's head. This has been done to inflame the spirit of licentiousness; as no one has presumed to stand forth to pay such a sum, the reward of course is nugatory; it however shews the temper of the times.

The busts of the Duke of ORLEANS and M. NECKER have been made in wax and carried about Paris in triumph: all the public places of amusement are shut up for fear of a riot and being destroyed, and several skirmishes have taken place among the troops in the different interests.

9

It is generally believed that the Count d' ARTOIS is fled to Spain; the QUEEN is supposed to be with the KING at Versailles. His MAJESTY does not appear to be so much disliked by the people, for it is not considered that the late measures were of his advising, but rather that he was persuaded to them by the QUEEN's junto.

Marshall BROGLIO, finding his army not sufficient to withstand the people in a general attack, and perhaps more from a fear that they might catch the spark of rebellion, and desert, if suffered to be widely distributed, has withdrawn himself with his whole force, and is entrenched at Versailles, in the front of the Palace, with a view to protect the Royal Family.

The Duke of ORLEANS is the popular character. The people have offered to declare him *Lieutenant General du Royaume,* or Lieutenant Governor of the Kingdom, which would place him at the head of public affairs. This offer the DUKE has declined.

All the houses belonging to the King's party have been more or less attacked and plundered. The servants have been forced to surrender up the musquets, pistols, and such other weapons, and join the multitude. In short the mob has risen to a degree of ferocity, unexampled in the annals of the country.

All the CORN MAGAZINES belonging to government near Paris have been broken open and stripped, and several large supplies coming from different parts of the country for the use of the King's army have been stopped. What adds therefore to the horror of the scene is, that in the midst of this licentiousness, while large quantities of corn and provisions are destroyed, several hundred thousands are perishing for want.

The roads about the country are become extremely dangerous and unsafe, from the deserters and rabble who have been freed from the public prisons. Several persons on the road to Calais have been robbed and ill treated.

M. NECKER is certainly gone to Geneva, though no one has heard of him since he left Versailles after his dismission. It was reported he came to England.

Lord MAZARINE who was freed from the Bastile, had nearly been stopped at Calais on Friday on his way here. He was with two other Gentlemen, his companions in misfortune, and being all extremely mean and shabbily dressed, were suspected for bad persons, and no one seemed desirous to embark in the packet with them. He was at length obliged to declare himself; on landing at Dover, his Lordship was the first to jump out of the boat, and in the fullness of his joy, and in gratitude to heaven for his deliverance, immediately fell on his knees, and kissing the ground thrice, exclaimed: 'GOD BLESS THIS LAND OF LIBERTY.'

The MARQUIS DE BIEVRE was the first person who arrived in London, in flying from the tumults of Paris. He arrived on Saturday at noon, and the accounts he brought with him were so unexpected, that they were at first not credited. He came, as most people have done who are since arrived, without any equipage whatever, or even a change of linen, so anxious were people in general to get away from France.

Besides the noblemen and their families who are already arrived in London, several more are hourly expected; among others, the PRINCESS DE LAMBALLE, MADAME DE CHABANE, the MARQUIS DE LA PALICE and his family &c.

July 22nd, 1789

THE BASTILE

A very curious report has gone abroad, of the Bastile's having been demolished during the late riots in Paris, originating in this idea, that because the wretched inhabitants of it have been released, the prison must necessarily be demolished. We can assure our readers that no such thing has, or could have happened, for to pull down this ancient fortress would be the work of long labour and time. Much damage has been done to it, and most of the gates have been pulled down, as well as some of the inside wards, the drawbridges, &c. but as to the main building, it stands as firm as ever.

The latest and best account we have of this horrid and gloomy dungeon, is in a small volume published last year at Mr. WALTER's, Printing-House Square, Blackfriars, and at No. 169, Piccadilly, entitled, MEMOIRS of HENRY MASERES DE LATUDE, who was confined the greatest part of 35 years in the Bastile, and was only released as late as the year 1784. This history is intermixed with many anecdotes of Madame de POMPADOUR, through whose intrigues he was imprisoned.

By LATUDE's descriptions it appears, that the walls are more than a fathom thick; the windows are barred in with 4 iron

11

grates, as well as the chimnies, and from the height of the walls to the bottom of the ditches measures, in many places, 500 feet.

In the whole, there is no history of this prison so authentic as the above, and it must be particularly interesting at the present moment.

The Bastille was indeed demolished, by a speculative builder who had been one of those who stormed it. The report above is a weakly-concealed puff for Mr Walter's business: he was, of course, the first proprietor of The Times.

The next extract shows The Times *at the peak of its enthusiasm for Liberty. The paper's Paris correspondent, perhaps still the Gentleman who wrote from Versailles, was however already taking a much blacker view of events than John Walter in London. The allusions to British politics are revealing. It was in 1789 that John Walter I began to receive his secret annuity from the Pitt administration; the rude references to the American war were salutes to Pitt's own powerful opposition to Lord North and George III. Charles James Fox, as 'Opposition Leader', and the Prince of Wales were already being assailed as Pitt's enemies by* The Times, *but the identification of Fox as the friend of French anarchy, as against Pitt, the man of constitutional order, had not yet emerged.*

The Times *was far-sighted in perceiving the association of foreign war with a restoration of royal power. In 1792 it was Brissot who hoped to use a declaration of war as a means of rallying royalists and even the King to the Revolution, and Robespierre who denounced this course as reactionary.*

July 23rd, 1789

The late convulsions in Paris were wholly owing to the change in the Ministry; for, though we must all lament the lives that have been lost in the contest, yet no one can doubt but much political good must proceed from it.

Look to your Inquisition—to your racks—to your tortures—and to your religious tyranny, O Spain! for the day of your emancipation cannot be at a very great distance—the right hand of your tyranny is cut off, and Freedom approaches to place her standard on the walls of your Inquisition!

A war with England is now the only hope left to the expiring embers of Absolute Monarchy in France. In that case, Spain might pour her troops into France, under pretence of protecting her from invasion—the House of Austria might afford more assistance, and a tremendous army overspread the whole country. Then, terms of peace patched up, those troops might attempt to recover the former system of Government.

Had the Queen of France made the conduct of the Queen of England her model—the Revolution of France would have slept perhaps for another century. She is said, when the tumult was over, to have uttered these words—"Happy Charlotte! thou art beloved and respected in a land of liberty—what shall I be?"

The next step that the new COMMONWEALTH of France, for it truly deserves that appellation, will probably take, is the establishment of TRIAL BY JURY, and, of course, a total abolition of Priestcraft, Torture, and the Bastile.

There is very little doubt but the French King will, by degrees, attempt to regain that despotic sceptre which has been wrested from his hands, and that Germany will afford him every assistance. But, on the other hand, it is to be considered that the great body of the people are for the new system—that every peasant in France is a soldier, and that the foreign troops would, in the end, meet with the fate of General Burgoyne at Saratoga in the year 1777, and of Lord Cornwallis at York Town in 1781.

July 28th, 1789

FRANCE

PARIS, JULY 22.

LIBERTY, which has for some time past, been the favourite hope of the FRENCH NATION, is a blessing of too solid a nature for the meagre understanding of that people. The very shadow of it seems to overwhelm them. They appear to have gained every point that they could possibly expect towards framing a new constitution, while the King has done everything in his power to co-operate with the public wish. It does not appear to us that he could have humiliated monarchy in a greater degree, unless he had laid his crown at the feet of the National Assembly. After the late submissions of the Sovereign, the renewed violences of the

13

people will operate to the obstruction of that liberty which they are intended to support. Licentiousness will beget anarchy, and the resulting confusions will go very far towards restoring the suspended powers of the French monarchy.

PARIS was again a scene of riot and confusion on Wednesday last, and the tumults would almost have justified the KING to retract the promises he had made the citizens on the Friday preceding, when he entered the city in procession. After the generous manner in which his Majesty conducted himself on that occasion, and the mutual vows made both by King and People, there should have been a general oblivion of past injuries to have made that union permanent.

Rewards have not only been put upon the heads of the KING's friends, by authority, but two more public executions have taken place on the persons of M. DE FOULON, and M. BERTHIER.

The former was a Cabinet Minister, and had been nominated, conjunctively with MARSHALL DE BROGLIO to the war department; the mob had sought after him at the time of the late riots in Paris, and to elude their vigilance, his friends had given out that he had died suddenly of an apoplexy. Since which he had used every effort to escape, but in vain. M. BERTHIER was Intendant of Paris, and was strongly suspected of having hoarded corn for the use of MARSHALL DE BROGLIO's army;—He was the person, who a short time since contradicted M. NECKER, when this Minister told the KING that a famine must be the consequence, if he suffered an army to approach Paris.

The most diligent search having been made for both these persons, they were apprehended, and on Wednesday last taken to the *Place de Greves*, where they were hanged publicly, their heads cut off, and afterwards carried on poles in triumph through the streets of Paris. . . .

Brussels is the general asylum for those persons who have fled. The public rewards, the executions that have already happened, and the want of protection from the KING, who indeed has not the power to give it, have driven all his most zealous friends from Versailles. The COMPTE D'ARTOIS is fled to *Nivelle*, near Brussels. His two sons, the DUCS DE ANGOULEME and BERRY, are at Brussels, with the PRINCE DE CONDE, the DUC DE BOURBON, the DUC DE ENGHIEN, and about twenty more of the first nobility of France.

The Provinces are in a state of rebellion from one end of FRANCE to the other. They seem no longer to consider allegiance to the King as a necessary part of their duty. . . .

The following extract was written in the office from various letters and newspapers from France. The Assembly debate referred to took place on August 4th.

August 11th, 1789

At the Paris Gate of St. Denis, the mob has hung and cut off the MAYOR's head, who was very injuriously and falsely accused of embezzling corn. The mob threatened to bring his head in triumph to Paris, but the Magistracy here have very properly sent a body of troops to prevent their passing the Barriers. There have been enough of sanguinary sights in Paris without this.

All these disorders accumulate the general misery. M. NECKER is so sensibly affected at these shocking transactions, that he makes no scruple everywhere to express his grief.

If anything can tend to alleviate our misfortunes and stop this alarming phrenzy, it is the hopes of having a constitution formed in less than a month. Besides this, the harvest is very fine and plentiful.

We now hasten to give the important deliberations of the NATIONAL ASSEMBLY on Tuesday last, which will ever be considered as a proud day in the annals of the French history.—Some of the Resolutions were very violently opposed.

The National Assembly did not break up till near two o'clock on Wednesday morning.

The following is an exact copy of their Resolutions.

A DECLARATION of the rights of men and citizens shall be inserted at the head of the NEW CONSTITUTION.

An equalization of taxes, to be paid from the present moment.

A renunciation of all particular privileges, whether of orders, towns, provinces, or Parliaments. All the provinces have very patriotically abandoned their privileges, and demanded a general uniformity of conduct throughout the kingdom, so that

15

they now form a sort of confederation for the preservation of the general safety.

Redemption of federal rights.

Suppression of the rights of the chace.—*Suppression des droits de chasse.*

The price of redeeming the incomes of the Clergy shall be placed to the profit of their benefices.

Suppression of mortmains, and all personal servitude.

The abolition of Lords of estates administering justice in right of their possessions.

The abolition of venal fees in courts of justice.

Justice to be gratuitously administered for the people.

Abolition of dove houses and warrens.—*Abolition des colombiers et garennes.*

Redemption of tenths and field rents.

Prohibition of creating in future any right of this kind, or other feudal rights.

Abolition of any substitute for Curacies, except in cities;

Augmentation prochaine des portions congrues;

Droit d'annates supprime;

Every citizen to have free admission to civil and military offices;

Suppression of the duties of delay *(de deport)* laid by Curates to Bishops in particular provinces;

Suppression des Jurands et Maitrises;

A plurality of benefices not to be allowed; (an example worthy the attention of the British Legislature.)

A Medal to be struck tocommemorate this memorable day;

A *Te Deum* to be sung in the King's Chapel, and throughout France, as soon as his Majesty shall have ratified these Articles;

LOUIS XVI. to be proclaimed, the RESTORER OF THE LIBERTY OF FRANCE.

During August, The Times *ran a series entitled 'Bastille Anecdotes'.*

August 13th, 1789

. . . One of the principles of this prison was,—that no one could ever enter its gates that would not gladly compound for instant death; and to prevent all the means of suicide was the first object of attention in the officers on the reception of a prisoner.

The personal examination to prevent any instrument of death from being secreted, is almost as ridiculous as the conduct of the customhouse officers of Japan, who are related to examine the very eggs, lest contraband commodities should be concealed in them:—It has been frequently known that powerful *lavements* and emetics have been instantly administered to a prisoner on his entrance, from the bare possibility that a small clasp knife might have been swallowed.—The sick are never bled till every other evacuation has been made in vain, and the patient is bound in such a manner as not to be able to stir, lest by an intentional motion of the arm the lancet might be made to reach an artery; and when a prisoner is indulged with the liberty of being shaved, the barber had a mode of tying on the shaving cloth, holding the head, and dispatching the ceremony, that the most resolute man could not move his neck, so as to produce an incision in a jugular vein.—The *fork* which accompanied the daily meals was of such soft materials that it bent double on the slightest pressure. No knife was allowed, and the meat was cut in small pieces by the person who served it.—When a prisoner was allowed to walk on the top of the prison, for the benefit of the air, he was accompanied by two soldiers, with bayonets fixed, who walked on each side of him, to prevent his throwing himself from the battlements.—When a book was granted from the Library, for this place possessed a library, the person who brought the volume counted the number of its leaves, in the presence of the prisoner, that he might not destroy himself by swallowing paper, such an attempt having been once made by some despairing inhabitant of the place. In short, the officers of the *Bastille* flattered themselves, that it was impossible for a prisoner to put an end to his existence, but by swallowing the fire that warmed him, or dashing his brains out against the walls that surrounded him.

August 15th, 1789

FRANCE

The following letter comes to us from an English Gentleman, who has been in Paris, and the neighbourhood, during the whole time of the present disturbances in France, and was an eye witness to most of the horrid barbarities that have been committed there. The style of it is easy and pleasant, and though it contains nothing materially new, yet it will afford much matter of observation.

Paris, August 10, 1789

According to promise, I seize the earliest opportunity to send you a more minute account of the various scenes through which I have been obliged to pass during the late memorable revolution.—Misrepresentation and visionary news, generally the offspring of common report, have never misled the credulous more than during the late struggle between expiring despotism, and triumphant freedom. The destruction of a few wretched monopolists, rendered the sacrifice of others familiar to those who had either too much fear to minutely scrutinize the tale of ignorance, or were too indolent to investigate rumours which carried contradiction with them. It was sufficient for such to know that half a dozen heads had been exposed upon pikes and lances, a house burned down, and the Bastille demolished, to believe every subsequent report, however monstrous and unnatural. Hence, through the medium of the Daily Prints, the avidity of the Public has probably been fed by a repetition of absurd events, which, having their source in imaginary facts, soon prove the futility of an easy faith.—It is however but just to allow, that, however barbarous and bloody the description of what happened to FOULON, BERTHIER, &c. may have been, it never could equal the reality.

The idea only of one man tearing from the mangled body of another pieces of flesh, and dipping the same into a cup, which was eagerly drained by the executioners of it, carries the mind into a wilderness of barbarity, from which, as from a dream of murder, it rests in a stupefaction of dread and horror; nor can reflection, in its momentary visit, reconcile the possibility of such an act existing, even in the wild fancy of disordered rage.

The savageness shewn to FOULON, a man of 70 years of age, was peculiarly horrid; he had retired to the country seat of M. de SARTINE, where he was discovered. The mob dragged him from thence to Paris behind a hay-cart bare-footed, with a collar of thistles and nettles round his neck. After walking a great way, and almost harrassed to death, at a place called *Villejuif, Foulon*

18

asked for a glass of water, instead of which, these tygers in human shape made him drink a glass of vinegar.

Arrived at the HOTEL DE VILLE in Paris, the mob demanded that he should be instantly tried, and that they would allow only one hour for it. They said it would be a novelty to see a man hung in France who had an income of 300,000 livres. But the MAYOR, and the Marquis de la FAYETTE, interceded strongly that he should have a legal trial, but the mob would hear of no such thing.

Tired with the intercession of the Magistrates, the mob threw stones at the windows of the Mansion House, and threatened to burn it down. At the same instant, a party of 3 or 400 rushed into the great hall, and seized the culprit. The Marquis de la Fayette fainted. FOULON was tied up to a beam in the Mansion House, and hanged. Being a large sized man, and very heavy, the cord broke; they fetched another—that broke likewise. The tygers then strangled him, and cut off his head, which they stuck on a pole. They then undressed him, and carried his body naked through the streets of Paris all night, sometimes laying the body down, and dancing round it like Cannibals.

It is, however, remarkable, that the money in his possession was all restored. There were found on him eleven Louis d'Ors, two gold watches, and a gold snuff-box, which were carried by some vagabonds, without even shirts, to the Magistrates.

The last execution which took place at *Saint Denis,* was scarcely less savage, though done when the frenzy of insatiable revenge began to cool; the head of the MAYOR, a man of three-score and upwards, with a wife and seven children, was carried about the streets, followed by his body, till day-break, and then sent to his family for interment. Such are the effects of oppression; careless in its hour of prosperity, whether the sword of revenge and awakened misery hang over it, so the temporary dictates of pride, lust and ambition be amply gratified. The great have before them an awful picture of what the poor can do; whilst the poor, on the other side, have at least the consolation to know, that, stripped of their gaudy pillage, the rich are the greatest objects of contempt and pity. . . .

The British remained absorbed by the unfolding of what one Times *correspondent was already calling 'the late Revolution'; many people assumed that a successful counter-stroke by the King was inevitable. This advertisement appeared on* The Times*'s front page on August 18th.*

August 18th, 1789

The ASSAULT of the BASTILE

Surrender of the Governor, and his Detachment—the Release of the Prisoners—and a most Extraordinary and Accurate

MODEL of PARIS.

ROYAL GROVE,

And ASTLEY's AMPHITHEATRE, WESTMINSTER BRIDGE.

THIS present EVENING will be performed a new Dance, (2d time) called
LA COQUETTE.
Composed by Sig. Marqui.

Various EXERCISES, by YOUNG ASTLEY,
His Pupils, &c. together with the astonishing Manoeuvres of his Horses.
ROPE DANCING, by Signior SPINACUTA.
A Comic Burletta, called THE BOOT-MAKERS.
The whole to conclude with an entire new and splendid Spectacle, founded on the Subject of
The FRENCH REVOLUTION,
From Sunday the 12th, to Wednesday the 15th of July,
both days inclusive, called
PARIS IN AN UPROAR!
Or, The Destruction of the BASTILE.
Displaying one of grandest and most extraordinary Entertainments that ever appeared, grounded on authentic Facts.
In the above Piece, the following Scenery, Machinery, &c. will be displayed;
First, a grand View of the Thuilleries Garden, from Pont Tournant, comprising La Place Louis XV.
Second, an Internal View of that magnificent and superb Promenade,
THE PALAIS ROYALE.

Third, External perspective View of the BASTILE, the Drawbridge, the Fossce, &c. shewing the manner of storming and taking the Bastile, by the Military and Citizens.

Fourth, a Picturesque View of the Inside of the BASTILE, leading from Mons. de Launay, the Governor's House.

Fifth, a Second View of the Caves, inside of the above Building.

Sixth, a Third View, Inside of the Strong Tower, comprising a Dark Dungeon, Remote Cells, &c.

The whole forming an exact Representation of that once tremendous Edifice.

And, in order to give a more conspicuous and just idea of the
CITY of PARIS,
A GRAND MODEL,
On an extraordinary Large Scale, including the Heart of that most capital City, from Le Pont Royale, in a direct Line on the River, to the Isle of Notre Dame (or St. Louis) exhibiting the River Seine &c.

1st. Pont Neuf; 2d, Pont au Change; 3d, Pont St. Michael; 4th, Pont Notre Dame; 5th, Petit Pont St. Jacques; 6th, Pont Charles; 7th, Pont du Bois; 8th, Pont Marie; and 9th, Pont de la Tournelle; together with the Churches, Squares, and other Edifices of the
CITY OF PARIS
Forming the most extraordinary Exhibition ever displayed on any stage.

The Music compiled from the French.

The Uniform of the Governor, Major Garde Criminelle, and Garde Francoise; Emblems of Liberty, &c. taken on the Spot.

The above Model of Paris is on a very large and extensive Scale, 50 Feet by 85, covering The whole Theatre. The Streets, Squares, Public Gardens, Halles of Public Amusement, innumerable Houses, &c. all of which are strictly conformable to that City, and have been the Study and Workmanship of an extraordinary number of Artificers, who have been employed day and night for some time past, on the occasion.

Mr. ASTLEY most humbly observes, that no expence or pains have been spared throughout this new and arduous undertaking; and he flatters himself, that the novelty of giving the City of Paris, so exact in every particular, on his Theatre at this moment, will be found very interesting to Ladies and Gentlemen who have visited Paris, as well as to those who have not.

The Doors to be opened at half past Five, to begin at half past Six o'Clock precisely.

Box 3s.—Pit 2s.—Gal. 1s.—Side Gal. 6d.

Places for the Boxes to be taken of Mr. Smith at the Amphitheatre.

†*† Ladies and Gentlemen instructed to Ride, and Horses broke for the Road or Field.

The Abbé Sieyès, quoted in the following extract was the author of the year's most influential pamphlet, 'Qu'est-ce que le Tiers Etat?', and later the constitutional expert of the Revolution.

August 20th, 1789

NATIONAL ASSEMBLY

The Assembly has at length gone through all the articles which are to form the principles of the New Constitution. It was near 3 o'clock on Wednesday morning before it broke up. There were only 19 articles passed.

The deprivation of the tenths of the Clergy was the article on which there was the most violent debates. The whole of that sitting was a scene of tumult and confusion; and for two hours before it broke up, not a single Member could be distinguished.

The principal speakers on this debate were the Abbe SYEYES, and the Abbe de MONTESQUIEU. The former is one of the most enlightened men of the present age, and much esteemed.

He said, that to deprive the Clergy of their tenths was nothing less than a robbery, and that it was dictated by avarice in the disguise of patriotism; that it was the property of the Clergy, and no tax on the proprietors of land, because the present possessors had deducted this tenth from the price of their purchases in calculating the sum they had paid for them.

The ABBE observed, that the tumultuous behaviour of the Assembly was a disgrace to their sittings, and that it was planned by a party, on purpose to drown the voice of reasoning. On being here interrupted by the noise of his opponents, he exclaimed, *Messeurs, n'est il permis de vous dire que des verites agreeables?*

Gentlemen, am I to be permitted to speak only such things as are agreeable to you?

The Abbe de MONTESQUIEU was not less urgent on the same side the question. He said, that the tenths of the Clergy had been held inviolate in all the stages of monarchy, from KING CHARLE-MAGNE to the present days.

This debate took place on the Monday evening, but was obliged to be adjourned on account of the turbulence of the Sitting. On Tuesday evening it took quite a different turn, as new as it was unexpected.

As soon as the Assembly met, eighteen Curates offered themselves to sign a paper, acknowledging their acquiesence of the suppression of the tenths of the Clergy, to the great astonishment of the other Members.

The Archbishop of PARIS and the Cardinal de la ROCHE-FOUCAULT rose to declare, in the name of all the Clergy, that they likewise gave their consent to the measure. They concluded by saying, that the Clergy threw themselves entirely on the justice of the nation, to bestow on them what compensation it should think fit for being thus deprived of their tenths.

The reason of this extraordinary and sudden liberality in the French Clergy was, that the majority in the National Assembly was full three to one against them. The best chance, therefore, was to throw themselves on the generosity of the country, and put the best appearance on what they could not prevent.

August 20th, 1789

We have now to announce, that the System to be established in FRANCE, and which is not only proposed, but actually determined on, is, that ALL THOSE TITLES, ON WHICH THE NOBILITY HAVE FOR SO MANY CENTURIES PLACED SUCH VALUE, ARE TO BE ABOLISHED, and the Antient Peerage of the Realm LEVEL-LED in common with all other distinctions.

The KING is to retain his title and his supremacy, as head of the people; but he is to be so restricted by the laws of the National Assembly, as to have the *shadow* without the *substance* of MONARCHY, the ostensible possession, whilst the people are the real proprietors of the Crown.

But the Aristocracy does not terminate here, the rights of

the Clergy are also abolished, and they have thrown themselves for protection on the new establishment.

And what further subverts the ancient constitution of France,—the private hereditary rights of whole Provinces are taken away,—rights of PROPERTY that centuries on centuries have guaranteed, *and* which every Court of Justice in the universe must allow to be LEGALLY, CONSTITUTIONALLY, and properly founded.

The plan agitated, which will be agreed to, is this:

The National Assembly propose that the King shall take possession of the ancient original manors, fiefs, and other territorial rights, which the crown when in want of money from *time* to *time* has SOLD, legally SOLD to the subject—and that his Majesty shall not allow to the present inheritors more than the original purchase money, so that the difference which time makes in the value of land, and the rise in consequence of improvement is not to be accounted for. This, at once, subverts all idea of equity in the national proceedings, and must in the end overturn the whole of their new system of Government, for in all enlightened countries, where CONSTITUTIONAL LIBERTY is held out as the basis of any new system, PRIVATE PROPERTY and HEREDITARY titles have even been held SACRED. England at this moment is a glorious proof of that fact, where the descendants of many an illustrious house, which has witnessed more than one revolution in both church and state, at this moment enjoy the titles and the estates of their ancestors.

There is one article of the nineteen already inserted in this Paper, containing the principles of the new constitution, which it is thought will meet with very great resistance in some of the Provinces. It is as follows:

"A National Constitution and Public Liberty, being more advantageous to the Provinces than the privileges which some enjoy, and whose sacrifice is necessary for the compact union of all parts of the Empire;—it is DECLARED, that all the particular privileges of provinces, principalities, countries, cantons, cities and commonalties, whether pecuniary or of any other nature, are abolished for ever, and shall remain confounded in the common right of all Frenchmen. . . ."

August 22nd, 1789

The Duke of DORSET's departure from PARIS has not tended to relieve the English nation from the jealousies of the French, they still have a strong idea of our having unfavourable views towards them.[1]

The more we consider the proceedings of the NATIONAL ASSEMBLY in FRANCE, the stronger we are in opinion, that the present revolution will never be accomplished without the loss of much blood. We never can believe, that the nobility will quietly submit to have their honors snatched from them, or that the *Pays d'Etats* will suffer to be stripped of their municipal powers, while they have a force within themselves to defend their ancient and just rights.

The ABBE de CALONNE[2] is gone to Spa, where he passes a great part of this time with the DEVONSHIRE family.

It is said to be the intention of the NATIONAL ASSEMBLY of France, on the election of their next President, to bring forward a Parish Priest into this eminent station, in order to stamp the complete triumph of equality, by placing him over the proud heads of the Church.

As a further example of the contempt of the KING's authority in France, a Member lately observed in debate that the Nation, and the Law should stand before his Majesty's name, for says he, *the King is nothing without the nation, and the nation may be everything without him.*

It would be extraordinary indeed if the people of France had continued in their admiration of the Duke of ORLEANS, as that Nobleman, before the late commotions, was held in very little respect, and was sometimes treated with marked insult in public.

The QUEEN of FRANCE was drove to the last extremity, when she endeavoured to appease the fury of the mob, by a *shew*

---

[1] The Duke of Dorset returned to France in time to witness the March on Versailles in October.

[2] Calonne had been Comptroller-General of Finances and founder of the Compagnie des Indes. He was removed from office on April 8, 1787. He corresponded with Pitt in subsequent years, and some of these letters were found in the famous 'iron chest' in the King's private rooms on November 20, 1792, whose contents precipitated the King's trial.

25

of that maternal duty to her own children, which she denied to a whole people over whom her husband was the *political* father. This the party of buff and blue[1] call *fine feelings!!!!!!*

The POPE suffers as much as the KING, by the present Revolution in France. His Holiness not only loses his pence, but his authority.

It is said that the FRENCH NOBILITY who have lately come over here from France, propose early in the ensuing winter to give a grand entertainment at the Pantheon, in gratitude for the protection which this country afforded them.

Doing and *overdoing* are very different matters,—and so it will be found in France; by taking too much, the people may not in the end gain any thing:—private property and hereditary honours were always held sacred in civilized countries, until the new National Assembly broke through those ancient barriers, and like *Wat Tyler* set up a system of levelling all distinctions.

The unpardonable strides which the French insurgents have taken to abolish all power but their own, will no doubt rouze the neighbouring arbitrary powers of Europe into a combination to restore the French Monarch to his throne, and the Nobility to their ancient rights. The provinces that are so plundered of their property, will no doubt join against the Olivierans, and perhaps the day is not distant when Louis the XVI, like Charles II, may be called back to all those privileges which his predecessor enjoyed.

As the National Assembly moved towards a new constitution, even a redefinition of society, The Times *gave more and more space to French news, sometimes two pages out of its meagre four. In the same issue as the following extract, the paper struggled to summarize its own 'editorial' view: 'Our readers mistake us if they suppose we are enemies to the REVOLUTION in FRANCE; while we decry the system which some hot-headed patriots wish to see adopted, we admire the heroism and public virtue which animate other parts of the nation.'*

---

[1] 'The party of buff and blue' was the Foxites. In 1788–9, during George III's madness, Pitt and the Queen were accused by the Foxites, who supported the Prince of Wales, of usurping royal power and prerogatives.

September 3rd, 1789

COPY OF THE DECLARATION OF RIGHTS AS FINALLY DECREED BY THE NATIONAL ASSEMBLY OF FRANCE

ON THURSDAY, AUGUST 27

THE Representatives of the French People, constituted in National Assembly, considering that ignorance, forgetfulness, or contempt of the Rights of Man are the sole causes of public misfortunes, and of the corruption of Governments, have resolved to set forth in a solemn Declaration, the natural inalienable, and Sacred Rights of Man, to the end that this Declaration, being constantly sent to all the Members of the Social Body, may perpetually remind them of their Rights and Duties; that the Acts of the Legislative and of the Executive Power, being at every instant liable to be compared with the object of every political institution, may be the more respected by them; and that the claims of the Citizens founded henceforward on simple and incontestible principles, may uniformly turn to the maintenance of the Constitution, and to the happiness of all.

In consequence, the National Assembly acknowledge and declare, in presence of, and under the auspices of the Supreme Legislator, the following *Rights of the Man and Citizen.*

ARTICLE I.

All men are born, and remain free, and equal in rights; social distinctions can only be founded on common utility.

ARTICLE II.

The end of every political association is the preservation of the natural and imprescriptible rights of man; these rights are liberty, property, security, and resistance to oppression.

ARTICLE III.

The principle of all Sovereignty resides essentially in the Nation; no body of men, no individuals can exercise any authority but what emanates expressly from it.

September 3rd, 1789

ARTICLE IV.

Liberty consists in doing whatever does not injure another; accordingly, the exercise of the natural rights of each man, has no other bounds but those which secure to other members of society the enjoyment of the same rights; these limits can be determined only by the law.

ARTICLE V.

The law should only prohibit actions injurious to society. Nothing can be prevented but what is prohibited by law; nor can any man be constrained to do what it does not ordain.

ARTICLE VI.

The law is the expression of the general will; all the citizens have the right of concurring personally, or by their representatives, in its formation; it ought to be the same for all, whether it protects or whether it punishes. All the citizens being equal in its eye, are equally admissible to all places, employments and dignities, according to their capacity; and without any other distinction, than that of their virtues and their talents.

ARTICLE VII.

No man can be accused, apprehended, or detained, but in cases determined by the law, and according to the forms which it has prescribed. They who solicit, expedite, execute, or cause to be expedited, any arbitrary orders, should be punished; but every citizen, summoned or apprehended by virtue of the law, should instantly obey, and he becomes culpable by resistance.

ARTICLE VIII.

The law should establish none but punishments strictly and evidently necessary; and no man can be punished but by virtue of a law established and promulgated prior to the offence, and legally applied.

ARTICLE IX.

Every man being presumed innocent, until he shall have been pronounced guilty, if it be deemed indispensable to apprehend him, every species of rigour not absolutely necessary for securing his person, should be severely prohibited by the law.

ARTICLE X.

No man can be disturbed in his opinions, *even religious*; provided their manifestation do not trouble the public *order* established by the law.

ARTICLE XI.

The free communication of thoughts and opinions is one of the most precious rights of man. Every citizen, therefore may freely speak, write and print, under condition of being responsible for the abuse of that liberty in cases provided for by the law.

ARTICLE XII.

The security of the rights of the man and citizen renders a public force necessary; that force then is instituted for the good of all, and not for the particular advantage of those to whom it is confided.

ARTICLE XIII.

For the maintenance of this public force, and the other expences of Administration, a common contribution is indispensable; this should be equally approportioned among all the citizens, [in] proportion to their abilities.

ARTICLE XIV.

Each citizen has the right, by himself, or his representative, to determine the necessity of the public contribution, freely to consent to it, to attend to its employment, and to fix the quota, the mode of imposition, the collection and duration of the same.

ARTICLE XV.

Society has a right to demand an account from every public agent of his Administration.

ARTICLE XVI.

Every society in which the guarantry of their rights is not secured, nor the separation of powers determined, is without a constitution.

These are the whole of the articles.

In Paris, revolutionary agitation increased as the Assembly debated at Versailles. The discussion on whether a royal veto ('negative') should be permitted or made suspensive rather than absolute — the second alternative was finally implemented — alarmed the democratic factions.

Shortly after the protest recorded below, the Café de Foi was raided and closed for a time. In 1794, just after Thermidor, there was a celebrated brawl in the Café de Foi when a boozer, imagining that democracy still reigned, addressed a general as 'toi'.

September 7th, 1789

RESOLUTION OF THE CAFE DE FOI, A NOTED COFFEE HOUSE FOR POLITICS NEAR THE PALAIS ROYAL AT PARIS

August 30, 9 o'clock at night.

The right of the *negative* is destructive of all liberty. It is about to plunge us again into that abyss of destruction from which we are only just extricated.

We must send a deputation to the NATIONAL ASSEMBLY to acquaint it of the intentions of the nation in this respect. Corruption and intrigue have gained over many Members of this Assembly,—we must therefore renounce them, send them back to their constituents and elect others. They would vainly plead the instructions of their representatives as their excuse;—but these instructions were formed in times of darkness when we yet groaned under the yoke of precedent and arbitrary power.

We have, however, broken those chains: the natural energy of man, who now enters on his rights, has succeeded a dastardly submission, and precedent has disappeared before the pure light of truth.

The present is therefore the first opportunity that the nation can properly dictate its instructions, and its will. The King is surrounded at Versailles; he must for his own safety commit HIMSELF and the DAUPHAIN to the love and protection of his faithful Parisian subjects. We will send six Deputies to the City, and twelve to the National Assembly at Versailles; but in order

30

to support the representations of these latter with greater energy, they shall be followed by a certain number of armed men, among whom shall be fifty, who shall compose the guard of the MARQUIS DE MIRABEAU.

We must immediately summon the 80 districts of Paris by the sound of the bell, and acquaint them with the decree of the Assembly at the CAFE DE FOI. . . .

.   .   .

POSTSCRIPT

We have just heard that the deputies of the Assembly of the CAFE DE FOI are returning from Versailles. They are expected back with the most eager impatience at the *Palais Royal,* where the crouds of people are immense, and heaped almost upon each other.

It is said that the NATIONAL ASSEMBLY received them with GREAT CIVILITY! ! !

September 24th, 1789

To the CONDUCTOR of the TIMES

SIR,

THE accounts that you furnish the public with, respecting the deplorable situation of the French, are such as must excite pity in every breast; but though we feel for the calamity of our fellow-creatures, as a nation, they are not entitled to any compassion.

The French have been long aiming at universal sovereignty; they are a restless, ambitious, and perfidious people; they have, for ages past, been the common disturbers of Europe, Asia, and America; they are ever upon the watch, and eagerly seize every advantage that presents itself in any nation; and they are the inveterate enemies of Great Britain.

Considering them in this great political view, I am of opinion, it would be greatly for the general good and peace of Europe, to annihilate the French Monarchy, and partition the kingdom.—The extinction of the Capetian race is but of small moment,—when put in competition with the general good and welfare of Europe, and the now subjects of France would be no losers. We often hear mention made of a lasting peace; but, whilst there exists a French Monarchy, there never will be a lasting peace.

31

There are powers who would gladly add some maritime consequence to their kingdoms, and there are those who would gladly augment what they now possess; but none of the partitioning powers would ever be of that consequence that France now is of, as a maritime power;—and Great Britain would naturally rise in her consequence.

The general character of the English is well known to be that of a liberal, peaceable nation, and always more ready to conciliate disturbances and mediate peace, than to promote discord and warfare; therefore she must ever be looked up to as a great maritime power,—but would be more so, were France partitioned; for at present, France is nearly equal to England in her marine; but, when joined by Spain, they are much superior. We withstood, in the last war, the combined force of France, Spain, and Holland; but I question much if we could again do it: and had their measures been equal to their power, in the last war, we must have been crushed.

I sincerely wish some abler pen would take up this subject, as it is most certainly a very interesting one.

I am, Sir, your's, &c.
ANTI-GALLICAN.

The Conductor was the publisher, John Walter I. William Finey was editor, but this was then an executive job combining something of the functions of a modern news editor and a chief sub.

Mr Astley, the showman, (see the advertisement on August 18th) was now facing competition. He hit back in another front-page advertisement.

October 5th, 1789

Mr. ASTLEY is just returned from Paris, with incontestible Proofs, that the WESTMINSTER BRIDGE Representation of the Siege, Storming, and Surrender of the BASTILE, on the 14th of JULY last, is strictly conformable to the particular circumstances of that day, and the only one so in London. Three places of Public Amusement having totally and differently represented the BASTILE, made Mr. ASTLEY anxious to give his Patrons the best authenticated informations. He can assure them, that no unmilitary-like combustibles, such as Roman Candles, Squibs, or Skyrocket Stars, were made use of. The idea of subduing a Fortress by such Amusements for Children is absurd, and of a piece with the rest of the business of the Love Story, &c. which never existed but in the Author's Brain in London.

Mr. ASTLEY has brought with him, finely executed in Wax, by a celebrated Artist in Paris, the Heads of Mons. DE LAUNY, late Governor of the Bastile, and Mons. DE FLE-SELLES, Prevot des Merchands of Paris; with incontestible proofs of their being striking likenesses. The Heads will be exhibited This Evening in the same manner as they were by the BOURGEOISIE and French Guards. He has also brought with him a complete Uniform of the ARMED CITIZENS, who are at this time exercising themselves in the further use of Arms in every part of Paris (his Riding School not excepted). Mr. ASTLEY will appear This Evening in the above Uniform, leading the Citizens and Soldiers to the Attack of the Bastile.

October 17th, 1789

Last night at *Astley's,* a young Lady (said to be from the country) was observed to hold her Mama's petticoat very fast during the Siege of the Bastile: the Old Lady rebuked her for timidity, and said, fye, fye, Nancy, 'tis only like partridge shooting — a certain proof that there is plenty of game round her Ladyship's manor.

Paris was now approaching its second insurrectionary explosion. The emigration of the wealthy was creating surprisingly wide unemployment in the capital, flour was running out and the King was massing loyal troops outside Paris. On October 5, the women of Paris marched to Versailles.

October 12th, 1789

FRANCE

CONFINEMENT
OF THE KING, QUEEN,
AND ROYAL FAMILY,
AND
THE ATTEMPT TO MURDER THE QUEEN

Independent of the awful crisis of his MAJESTY's late illness, there never was a moment which excited the anxiety and attention of all ranks of people, so much as the present revolution in France: it is not now merely the disputes of the NATIONAL ASSEMBLY, and the new modelling of the French Constitution, which claim the attention of our countrymen, in common with all Europe, but the very lives of the ROYAL FAMILY of FRANCE, and the race of a whole monarchy, are at stake.

At this moment, the fate of Europe depends on the actions—of A BARBAROUS and UNRESTRAINED MOB!—a mob, which has shewn itself so licentious, that the country which claims it, blushes at its cruelties. The MURDER of the QUEEN has been attempted in the dead of night, while she was in her slumber, and unprepared to appear before the tribunal of her Maker,—at a time of all others the most awful and barbarous, because the most sacred and inoffensive.

Had the attempt succeeded, what must have been the consequence? or indeed, what may not now be the consequence? for her life is still in danger;—a QUEEN, who is the sister of the EMPEROR and the Grand Duke of TUSCANY, and allied to the Houses of SPAIN, SARDINIA, NAPLES, and almost all the Princes of ITALY.

· · ·

The circumstances of the entertainment at VERSAILLES have not yet been accurately stated. It was given within the Palace by the King's express permission, and when the desert was served up, their MAJESTIES entered the hall with the DAUPHIN, which inspired such enthusiasm among the officers and troops, who were admitted within to drink their healths, that they entered

34

into an oath, and sanctified it by kissing their sabres, to continue faithful to the Royal family. The QUEEN was so much affected at the sight, that she shed tears.

The Royal Family a short time afterwards appeared at the balcony of the *Cour de Marbre,* when they were again saluted with shouts of—*Vive le Roi,—Vive la Reine.* The evening concluded with the greatest mirth and harmony.

The disturbances in Paris, on hearing of these proceedings became so general on Monday last, that all the districts of the capital were summoned, and the MARQUIS DE LA FAYETTE was ordered to proceed immediately to Versailles, at the head of a large body of troops, and bring the KING under his guard to Paris. On receiving these orders, the Marquis DE LA FAYETTE remonstrated, saying, that he would first go thither attended by only a few of the Magistrates and some guards, and make his report of the necessity of a reinforcement.

This soon got wind abroad, and the mob ever ready to catch at anything which could bear an unfavourable construction, insisted that the Marquis de la Fayette, and the Mayor, whom they likewise suspected, were gained over to betray them. While this suspicion was circulating, another party erected two gallows in the *Place de Greves,* and threatened to hang them if the orders were not instantly complied with.

We must own that we have never been particularly struck, or convinced of those heroic feats of valour which the Marquis de la FAYETTE is said to have performed in America. In a former number of this paper, we gave the outlines of this Nobleman's public character, and we think the event has greatly confirmed our opinion. In the present instance, M. DE LA FAYETTE betrayed a pusillanimity of character unworthy of his high rank and military capacity. He was conscious that the orders he received were treacherous and unjust, by his first refusal to obey them; but the threat of the mob struck such terror into him, that he chose rather to obey their commands, and bring his KING in ignominy to Paris, than risk his own safety by refusing their commands.

In the evening of Monday therefore M. de la FAYETTE set out for Versailles, at the head of 20,000 of the Parisian Guard, and attended by several of the Magistrates of the City of Paris. He had been preceded in the morning by about 8000 persons, chiefly Fishwomen (*Poissonniardes*) accompanied by their Chief, who has the appellation of, *Queen of Hungary.*

October 12th, 1789

The troops did not arrive at Versailles till late in the evening, and were under arms the whole night, partly to take their stations about the Palace and secure the avenues, and in order to repel any attack from the troops posted within.

At two o'clock on Tuesday morning, a considerable number of the persons who were habited in women's dresses, but as it since appears, were many of them guards, having gained the outward entrances of the castle, forced their way into the Palace, and up the staircase leading to the Queen's apartment, with an intent to seize and murder her; fortunately, a greater number than usual of the King's body guard were ordered to sleep in the Anti-chambers leading to it, and to be particularly vigilant against any alarm.

The disturbance soon roused them to arms, and the first body who made the approach were fired on, and 17 killed on the spot. The rest terrified at the fate of their companions, instantly retreated, and every thing resumed a tolerable state of quietude till the morning.

The PARISIAN troops having demanded entrance at the Palace, it was refused, and they received a fire from the regiment of the KING's Body Guard, who defended the approach of the Palace. A few troops and some women who had mixed in the crowd, fell on the first fire, which was immediately returned by the Parisian Guard. The action becoming more general, the Count de LUSIGNAN, Commandant of the Regiment of Flanders, ordered his troops to fire, which they refused to, and laid down their arms. The King's Body Guard finding themselves over-powered, took to flight, and the troops then forced the entrances of the castle, and were only prevented from entering the Palace in a body, by the management and command of the MARQUIS de la FAYETTE. There is reason to believe, that had this happened, the KING, QUEEN, and Royal Family would have fallen victims to their fury.

The MARQUIS was soon after introduced to the KING, with some of the Magistrates of Paris, and communicated the desire of the city that he might conduct his MAJESTY and the ROYAL FAMILY thither. On being assured of protection, the KING made no hesitation to comply with the request, well knowing that it would not have availed him. Orders were therefore immediately given for the Royal Equipages to be got ready, and their MAJESTIES with the DAUPHIN, MONSIEUR, and the KING's AUNTS, proceeded to town, with their attendants, in a procession of eighteen carriages, attended by the Marquis DE LA FAYETTE, and about 5000 Guards. His MAJESTY was in the first carriage with a Nobleman of his Household,—the QUEEN and DAUPHIN in the second.

The road from Versailles was so thronged by the mob, that notwithstanding 50,000 of the Parisian troops had been sent out to keep the way clear, the Royal Family were eight hours in reaching the *Hotel de Ville,* though only a distance of twelve miles. This tedious journey could have been rendered only more painful, by the thoughts of being led CAPTIVES in triumph to the city of Paris, and the fear of what was to follow.

Being arrived at the *Hotel de Ville,* the Royal Family stopped there near two hours. The KING was shewn into the Great Hall, where he was harangued by Monsieur de ST. MERY, who assured his MAJESTY of his safety,—that he had only been conducted to Paris for his better security, and that he would find himself more happy among his *Loyal Children* there, than he had been at Versailles. To all this his MAJESTY seemed to pay but little attention. The Royal Family were then conducted to the old ruinous Palace of the *Thuilleries,* which has not been inhabited since the days of LEWIS the XIV, and where nothing was prepared for their reception.

In the affray at VERSAILLES, the King's body guards behaved most nobly. In the slaughter which happened there, about 50 of the Parisian troops and mob were killed, and 30 of the King's guards cut to pieces. Eighty of them were taken prisoners, and brought to Paris, the rest saved themselves by flight.

This regiment is peculiar to any other, being composed, both privates as well as officers, of persons of the second order of nobility in France. The heads of those who were slain, were carried in triumph to Paris, and shewn about the streets on tent poles, as a further specimen of the savageness and ferocity of a Parisian mob.

On Wednesday last, all the districts of Paris met early in the morning, and orders were given to surround all the avenues of the THUILLERIES, which had been only defended the preceding night by a common guard. A thousand troops were immediately ordered on that duty, and all the gates of the Palace are further secured by a train of CANNON to prevent any surprize or escape.

Wednesday at noon, being the Court day, their MAJESTIES received all the foreign Ministers in the Palace. The KING looked

37

uncommonly dejected, the QUEEN was in tears the whole time, and only talked a few words to the Imperial Ambassador. The sight was uncommonly gloomy and affecting, and the Court broke up after a short time.

In the evening the districts of PARIS passed a resolution, that the regiment of the KING'S BODY GUARD should be immediately broken, and never more revived. That in future his MAJESTY should be guarded by citizens, instead of soldiers.

During these proceedings at Paris, the National Assembly at Versailles could not be supposed able to transact much business. They, however, came to two Resolutions on Wednesday, which it was supposed would be the last day of their sitting there.

The purport of these resolutions were,—

That the National Assembly should adjourn to Paris; and,

That its meeting should never be INSEPARABLE from the King's place of residence.

October 14th, 1789

... It requires no great deal of penetration to foresee what will be the consequence of the removal of the National Assembly to Paris;—the precious opportunity of the KING'S imprisonment must not be lost; and, as there is no power to refuse the laws which the Parisians are disposed to make, so we may shortly expect to see the Constitution of FRANCE dressed, like a fine Lady, with a new suit of cloaths in the very pink of the Parisian fashion,—of much shew, but little intrinsic worth or durability.

But, is it likely to be supposed, that the Provinces will yield to the decrees of the National Assembly, dictated under the influence and awe of the City of Paris?—Certainly not;—and hence we may presume, that many Provinces already much discontented at what has been done, will resist the execution of them; for which would be so base as to suffer a suspicion of being governed by laws imposed under any other than a free, unbiassed legislation.

In our opinion, the late French revolution is only preparatory to a third, though at a less interval of time than between the first and second. The Government cannot last long as it is at present, nor can we suppose that even the Provinces of FRANCE will suffer their KING to be a State puppet in the hands of the Parisians,— still less, that foreign powers will see it with a silent voice.

38

The prophecy, though intelligent, was not fulfilled. Paris did not dictate to the Assembly, which now embarked on its great course of reform: the nationalization of church property, the abolition of nobility, the reform of land tenure and the civil constitution of the clergy. The captive court manoeuvred and intrigued, but there was no foreign or provincial intervention to rescue it.

The Times *continued to predict its 'third revolution', and viewed events with deepening pessimism. The following leader is a pinchbeck version of Burke's profound alarm.*

June 30th, 1790

THE
ABOLITION OF TITLES IN FRANCE

The NATIONAL ASSEMBLY of FRANCE, in restoring what they call the rights of man to their country, seem to be depriving it of those distinctions which form the connecting powers, and consequently are the rights of society. Abstract ideas of perfection may suit very well with the principal system of the closet politicians, but will never apply to the nature of man, either in his individual or social capacity. The *Utopia* of Sir Thomas More and the Republic of Plato, may serve to amuse the mind, as pleasing fictions of unexisting perfection; but there never was a society, and, without exercising any unjust spirit of censure on human nature, we may venture to assert, there never will be a society in which the principles of those eminent and amiable theorists can be reduced to practice.

If we consider mankind in every form of social compact, from the earliest periods of history, through all the various changes and modifications of society, to the present moment, we shall see that distinctions, and we may add, distinctions of rank and honour, have universally prevailed. Some of the Grecian Democracies, with the history of which, we believe much fable is intermixed, affected to preserve a strict equality among all their citizens; but, even supposing the system of Lycurgus to have existed, which we very much doubt, in all the rigour it is handed down to us,—still we find the two most leading distinctions of society involved in it,—which is Freemen and

39

June 30th, 1790

Slaves.—But the conclusion of the Greek Republics evidently proves, that such a system could not hold together for the continuance of a great society. The Government of the Shepherd Kings in the East, had its distinctions;—the Gothic institutions of the North, from whence modern Europe has borrowed its best forms, were founded on a difference of rank among their people,—and the Islands of the Southern Pacific Ocean, lately discovered by our Navigators, offer the same picture of distinct and separate orders. In short, it does not appear to be consistent with the nature of things, that a Government, supposing it even to arise out of the Forest, can subsist upon principles of entire and undeviating equality among the individuals who compose it.

How then is it possible, that an extensive Empire, nourished in luxury, and the characteristic of whose people is vanity, can step at once from a state of refinement, which borders on depravity, to those principles of policy, which nations emerging as it were from barbarity, find too simple for their adoption.

That the distinction of ranks in France, has been carried to a ridiculous, an unnatural, and impolitic height, is readily acknowledged;—but, if to destroy any part of a system, because it has been abused, be a principle of their present Government,—they will lay the axe to the root of religion itself,—and when they annihilate coronets and titles, they must on the same principle level their churches with the ground.

We have continually foretold, that the mad spirit of change now prevalent in France, will, in the end, destroy its own object,—and we are not afraid to repeat the prophecy. Reformation is certainly necessary; but to be effectual it must be slow in its progress and moderate in its exertions. Violence will defeat it,—and will operate like the spirit of Brother Jack, in the Tale of a Tub,—who, in the ardour of his zeal to separate the embroidery from the coat, *tore the cloth along with it.*

This gloom was not yet shared by wide sections of the British population, more stirred and inspired by the early years of the Revolution than any other nation in Europe. A proliferation of revolutionary and radical clubs appeared.

CELEBRATION
OF THE
FRENCH REVOLUTION

Yesterday being the day appointed for the celebration of the Anniversary of the Revolution in France, which began on the 14th of July 1789 by the demolition of the Bastile, a very numerous society of Gentlemen of the first distinction, with Earl STANHOPE, as their Chairman, met at the Crown and Anchor Tavern to dine.

Though we do not agree in opinion with these Gentlemen on the principles of the French Revolution, nor that the people of France are likely to become more happy under their present REPUBLICAN GOVERNMENT, we nevertheless beg leave to testify our approbation at the motives which produced this zeal in the cause of freedom, for if their judgment misleads them, it is at least from a pure conviction that it is right.

.   .   .

Lord Stanhope then gave a toast, in the name of the Stewards, nearly as follows:—"Mr. Sheridan, and the worthy Patriots of Great Britain and Ireland who have defended the French Revolution."

This brought up Mr. Sheridan, who desired to return thanks to the Stewards and the Company for drinking his health. He said it was the most flattering acknowledgment he could receive, as a testimony of approbation of his public conduct, and he aspired to no higher honour. He said, that although he had the misfortune to differ in opinion from several of his most respectable friends on this subject, he trusted that he should always continue in the sentiments he had avowed. There never was a period [as] fortunate for the liberties of mankind, as the present. He begged leave to move a resolution to the following purport.

"That this meeting do sincerely rejoice in the establishment of the Revolution in France, and at the cordiality which subsists between the two nations."

Mr. Horne Tooke said, that although he was a most cordial friend to the revolution in France, yet he begged leave to differ

41

in many points from Mr. Sheridan. He compared France, previous to the Revolution, to a state ship whose rudder was unmanageable, and therefore it was become necessary to lay down a new keel. But in England, it was not so. We have, says Mr. Tooke, with great spirit and ingenuity, a vessel, *whose timbers are yet sound.*

Here a most violent hissing ensued, and the room became a scene of anarchy and confusion for near an hour, similar to what we have lately seen in France. In vain did Mr. Tooke request that the company would patiently hear him to the end, and then give their approbation or disapprobation as they thought his speech deserved.

Lord Stanhope at length rose and called to order, and for a moment the noise subsided—Mr. Newman, the Sheriff, then got on the Table to inform the company, that he had asked Mr. Tooke in the beginning of the day, whether he came to there to celebrate the French Revolution, to which he had not received a satisfactory answer.

This speech only encreased the tumult, and from the noise at the lower end of the room, something resembling the Bulls and Bears at the Stock Exchange, it was evident that persons had been sent to the meeting to throw it into confusion.

At length Mr. Tooke was suffered to proceed. He said he had often in his younger days feared women, but that he should never learn to fear men. He did not rise to oppose the motion, but to add something to it. He was sorry that many of the company seemed unwilling to hear the truth from him, though he should persist to ask, whether it were not useful to the public to understand the real state of things, and to make a difference between a ship whose keel is foul, and one whose keel is still sound, though it might want repairs, which he acknowledged it did in many parts.

Mr. Sheridan replied to Mr. Tooke, and said he should not disturb the harmony of the meeting by entering into any dispute with him, but he begged to leave to say, he had misrepresented the whole of what he had said. He then requested permission to drink—The Earl of STANHOPE.

Lord Stanhope said—he should ever remain a friend to civil and religious Liberty.

A Resolution of Mr. Horne Tooke's was then passed—"That this country has not so arduous a task to perform as the French have had, and that it has only to renovate and improve the ancient principles of the Constitution."

It was now nine o'clock, and the wine getting, as is usual at all public meetings, above the understanding, reason gave way to this powerful adversary, and much noise and confusion ensued.

The company was extremely numerous, but the dinner was not near sufficient for the company, or the price that was paid for it. Its scanty appearance was a discredit to the House.

A large piece of the Bastille stonework was brought in and laid on the table before Lord Stanhope, as a memento of the destruction of that prison.

The Stewards all wore the National Cockade of blue, red, and white.

For the first anniversary celebrations of the Revolution, the paper despatched 'a Gentleman concerned in The Times . . . *for the purpose of bringing, by express, a full and authentic statement of whatever happens on that day worthy of remark.' The correspondent failed, however, to get his story through on time.* The Times *had to use another source.*

July 19th, 1790

FRANCE

THE GRAND CONFEDERATION

PARIS, *July 15*

The following extract of a letter from Paris, dated on Thursday Morning, comes by the way of Dieppe. The Packetts from Calais have been detained there by contrary winds, the French Mail therefore, which should have arrived yesterday, is still due.

The situation of the buildings erected on the CHAMP DE MARS *has been already given in this paper of Saturday, and on comparing it with the other parts of this letter, we find it to have been extremely exact. It was calculated that about 400,000 persons were assembled, who had a full sight of the Altar where the Civic Oath was administered. The letter then states as follows:*

43

July 19th 1790

"All the streets which communicate with the *Champ de Mars* were furnished with scaffolds, for the use of those who had not the privilege of being present on the spot.

"The first who entered the field were deputations from various artists, bearing emblematic devices of the destruction of TYRANNY, and the establishment of FREEDOM. That which emphatically demonstrates the superiority of France to England, was a procession of journeymen *Printers* displaying a magnificent banner, on which was written, in letters of gold, 'A FREE PRESS is the BASIS of LIBERTY.'

"Each of the sixty districts of Paris also bore emblems suitable to the occasion.

"But when the captors and demolishers of the Bastile appeared, such united shouts of joy and triumph were perhaps never heard. Conceiving that dreadful prison to have been one of the grandest engines of despotism and cruelty, the multitude were frantic in the expression of their joy, when they beheld those sturdy arms that levelled it with the dust.

"*Fayette*, now *Mr. Moitier*, was received with the distinguished exclamation,—*vive notre* General!

"Excepting such trifling accidents as are usual when prodigious multitudes are assembled, I have heard of no disaster whatever, but one, and that arose from the bursting of a cannon, on firing a Royal Salute, when the King entered the field. It is reported that five or six men were killed on this occasion.

"His Majesty came on the ground precisely at half past twelve o'clock, and was escorted to his seat by M. *Moitier*, (late *la Fayette*) M. *Bailli*, the Mayor of Paris, and a few officers of the National guard. The Queen followed, and was conducted to a box at some distance from where his Majesty sat. M. *d'Orleans* mixed with the other representatives of the Nation, and had no particular honours paid him.

"The infinite complacency and satisfaction visible in the countenance and deportment of the KING and Mr. D'ORLEANS sufficiently refute the lamentations of the *Anti*-Revolutionists in England. It was impossible for men to acquiesce with greater apparent cordiality in the ceremonies of this day than they did. There may be hypocrisy in this, but hypocrites are worthy detestation, not pity.

"The ceremony commenced by the President and Members of the National Assembly taking the Civic oath.

44

"*I swear to be faithful to the* NATION, *the* LAW, *and the* KING, *and to maintain with all my powers, the Constitution decreed by the* NATIONAL ASSEMBLY *and accepted by the* KING.

"The Members of the National Assembly were all dressed in black.

"The KING then approached the Altar and said:—

"*I, King of the French, swear to the Nation to employ all the power which is delegated to me by the Constitutional Law of the State, to maintain the Form of Government decreed by the* NATIONAL ASSEMBLY, *and accepted by me, and to enforce the execution of the Laws.*"

"After this mutual compact between the King and the people, *Te Deum* was sung by a more numerous congregation than ever assembled since the *Te Deum* of the *Jews* for their deliverance from *Pharoah* and his *Host*.

"It not being practicable to recite the words, of the civic oath but to the President, the Members of the National Assembly were at liberty to substitute what form of words they thought proper.

"Each Member, on passing the Altar, lifted up his hand and exclaimed—"*That* I Swear!"—A fine field for *mental reservation!* ample scope for *jesuitical perversiom!*—I the Abbe *Maury* will exert all the powers of my soul to restore the *old Constitution,* and overwhelm with destruction this accursed democracy; *that* I swear.

"You will pardon my entering into all the particulars of this august confederation, till the next Messenger leaves Paris. What with the difficulty of being strictly accurate on every point, and the fatigue of the day, I am more inclined to sleep than to write.

"I cannot, however, deny myself the pleasure of mentioning a very laughable part of the procession. The Colliers led one of their comrades in a *band, black mantle,* and in *chains,* to represent the destruction of *Ecclesiastical Tyranny.* The fellow's droll appearance excited much mirth among the spectators.

"Of the Mottos on the banners, you will be best pleased with the following—*Libre ou Mourir,* Freedom or Death—*Les Esclaves du Despotisme sont devenus les Enfans de la Liberte,* 'The Slaves of Despotism are become the Children of Liberty.'

"When I consider that in the vast dominions of France, the same spectacle of confederation was yesterday exhibited, the same prayers offered up to Heaven for the blessings of the new

Constitution, and the same vows to perish in its defence, I am not extravagant, I hope, in my opinion, that from the creation to the present moment, the Sun never beheld any thing more interesting and sublime. ADIEU."

P.S. Every precaution was taken to prevent *tumult* and *massacre*. All suspected places were searched. Not a carriage to be seen in the streets,—canes, swords, and every sort of weapon interdicted. Not even the Flower Girls were permitted to impede passengers by pressing them to purchase *nosegays*.

July 24th, 1790

NEW PARISIAN DRESSES

FIRST LADIES' DRESS

The hat *a la jardiniere,* with blue ribbons, which come thrice round it, forming a knot behind, and a cockade before, with two white feathers. The hair dressed in a mass of curls, which fall on the bosom. The neck-kerchief of white gauze, in the middle of which is stuck a nosegay *(bouquet)*.

The piece of white gauze in folds.

The robe of blue taffetas, bordered with white. The petticoat of white linen, encircled with two red ribbons, and bordered with red taffetas. The shoes blue.

SECOND LADIES' DRESS.

The sides of the hat are of *jonc*. The crown, which is very high, is covered with crimson taffetas, with crimson knot, and a white feather. Under the hat a cap *(collinette)* of linen, in small folds.

The hair dressed in curls, falling down.

The neck-kerchief projecting.

The robe of striped taffetas, the large stripes are of deep green, and the small of a more delicate green. Before the robe a border of white taffetas, forming small triangles.

The girdle of red taffetas.

The petticoat of white taffetas, edged with green taffetas.

The shoes green.

46

FRANCE

PARIS, *March 8.*

It is reported that the army of the malcontents is preparing to march into the kingdom, and that it extends already from Landau to Weissembourg. But it is not their intention to act without support, and their hope is, that the first strong town they arrive at will throw its gates open, and receive them amicably. They are employed at present in procuring provisions along the Rhine. Their principal object is to become masters of Lorraine and Champagne.

To defray the expences of this army, about fifteen or twenty millions of livres have been collected in London, at Genoa, in Switzerland, and in Germany. It is said that M. de Calonne is the person who has procured this money.

M. de Rochambeau, or M. de Bouille, will be appointed Commander in Chief of the army. We have already 16,000 men on the frontiers, 12,000 infantry and 4,000 cavalry.

The King has notified to those Princes who have encouraged his rebellious subjects, and given an aslyum to French fugitives, that they may be sure of retaliation; and that he will not suffer any power to disturb the new Constitution which he, in concert with his people, has just established.

M. de la Fayette has just published a Letter tending to vindicate his conduct on the 28th of February, at the Thuilleries, and to contradict a report that he had been appointed Commander of the interior Establishment of the King.

The *Club des Jacobins* subscribe every month above 40,000 livres, the greater part of which money is to encourage seditious mobs, riots, and tumults, in order to keep the hatred of the nation against Monarchy alive, and by that means to be enabled to establish a rank Republic. The disturbances at the Thuilleries are attributed to their secret manoeuvres.

Mr. Beckford is almost the only foreigner here of consequence. He has given the Parisians several splendid balls, for which he has been abused in the public Papers. Insults and the most gross licentiousness are now considered as proofs of the existence of the Liberty of the Press. Nothing is sacred—nothing escapes calumny.

Late on the night of June 20th, the Royal Family made their carefully-planned attempt to escape and reach the Austrian armies at the frontier. The King and Queen were recognized the following evening at Sainte-Ménehould, and caught at Varennes.

June 27th, 1791

... The escape was certainly made through one of the private doors of the palace; it is believed through a passage leading from the pavillion in which the Queen slept, and from which there is a private communication to the garden. This avenue had no sentry placed over it. It is said that the Royal Family got into their carriages at the *Pont Royal,* a short distance from the palace. It is further believed that several officers of the King's former body guard attended at the escape, and that some of them followed the Royal carriages at a little distance dressed in liveries; for about fifty persons immediately in the confidence of their Majesties are missing, and several have left the capital within the last fortnight. But the escape was most secretly contrived and as admirably executed, as human wisdom could have suggested, for relays of horses were stationed on the road all the way to French Flanders, in order to facilitate the journey. It is suspected that M. de BOUILLE, who commands in French Flanders, assisted the escape through the garrison towns under his authority.

The news of the escape became generally known through Paris about nine in the morning, which, as it may be supposed, created great confusion; the national guards were immediately ordered under arms, and double sentries were posted at all the gates in the town, with orders to prevent any person from passing or repassing, and the alarm bell was rung; couriers were likewise dispatched by the municipality to different parts of the country with the news, and desiring the citizens to be on their guard whom they suffered to pass through their towns. Many faces wore a countenance of surprize, several carried visible marks of terror, and a general dismay prevailed among the democrates. The mob, ever ready to exercise the uncontrolled RIGHTS of MEN, made a mock parade of the King's Arms in the market places, and, dashing them and the figure of a crown to the ground, they trampled upon them, crying out—"since the King has abandoned what he owed to his high situation, let us trample upon the ensigns of royalty!"

· · ·

But by a courier which left Paris in the night of Thursday, and arrived yesterday at the FRENCH AMBASSADOR's we are sorry to learn . . . that his Majesty and the Royal Family have been captured on the road to METZ in *Lorraine.* They had reached St. MENEHOUD, one of the last post towns in *Champagne,* where they arrived on Wednesday afternoon, having travelled 156 English miles. Here they were recognized by the Post Master, as they were changing horses, who instantly sent an express (cross roads) to the municipality of *Varennes,* 26 posts from Paris, and 10 from Metz in Lorraine, and at this last place they were arrested by the *Garde Nationale,* who sent a courier to the National Assembly for instructions how to act.

This news arrived at Paris on Thursday afternoon, while the Assembly was sitting, who immediately appointed three Commissioners, Messrs. *Barnave, Pethien de Villeneuve,* and *la Toure-Maubourg,* to go to *Varennes,* to bring back the King.

The suspicion of M. de BOUILLE's having laid a plan to favour the Royal Family's escape through French Flanders is confirmed, and had they passed *Varennes,* they had been safe, for he had sent detachments of men as far as there to conduct them out of the kingdom. The National Assembly therefore on Thursday night decreed, that he should be ARRESTED. M. de la FAYETTE has justified himself of the imputation of being privy to the King's escape.

It evidently appears from the above, that the KING intended to escape to METZ, the capital of the Elector of that name, where the Chiefs of the Counter Revolution now are.

June 30th, 1791

. . . No sooner was the Royal Family of France brought back to their former situation in Paris, than the KING and QUEEN were put under a strong guard in the *Thuilleries,* and made CLOSE PRISONERS. Though lodging under the same roof, they are debarred every comfort of each other's society, and CONFINED in SEPARATE APARTMENTS, with sentinels placed to watch over their conduct, and preclude them from holding the slightest intercourse. The KING is to be made a prisoner for life, and the QUEEN will probably not meet a happier fate, unless, indeed, she should be returned to her brother the *Emperor.* Had not the

National Guards taken the most diligent precautions to keep off the mob as she entered Paris, the Legislature might have been spared the trouble of debating on the mode of punishing her Majesty, for she was threatened to be torn to pieces. The mob betrayed every sign of intended violence, and hooted the Queen as she passed through the streets. The procession into Paris was otherwise conducted with great regularity.

July 5th, 1791

The NATIONAL ASSEMBLY of France are following closely the steps of the long Parliament in this country—and their grand aim is no doubt to *take off their King*, and put an end to all Royal Authority. This done, it may probably follow that the Chief Gaoler of Paris will then, at the head of the army, declare himself Protector of the Realm, and under that title, rule the deluded people with *a rod of iron*; which, for the sake of popularity, will be stiled a Democracy. But like our tyrant *Oliver*, he will soon become universally hated, and the people watch and wish for an opportunity to return to their old system of Government.

Though the public attention is almost absorbed in the situation and circumstances of the Royal Family of France, there is another event which gives a very peculiar example of the present and very altered state of the temper of that kingdom. We mean the very distinguished honours which are paid to the remains of VOLTAIRE.

This man, who was the professed apostle of infidelity—whose writings make a mockery of every religious faith upon the face of the globe—who lived a blasphemer and died blaspheming—who had no one virtue, and whose genius was the powerful instrument of vice, receives the posthumous veneration of a people whom he had corrupted; and who, in the madness of infidel fanaticism, pay such honours to his remains as have never yet been offered to the friends, to the instructors, the illuminators, the fathers of the human race.—The inhabitants of Paris, as if that city did not contain enough of living impiety, are, under the influence of their Legislatqre, preparing to receive the desiccated carcase of their impious philosopher, dislodged from a stolen grave, with all the pomp, and re-inter it with all the solemnity which the most enthusiastic affection of a grateful

50

people could display in honour of patriot Kings,—*Deliciae humani generis.*

July 18th, 1791

RIOT AT
BIRMINGHAM

Anniversary meetings in commemoration of the French Revolution, we have long declared to be highly dangerous to the peace of this country, the inhabitants of which differ, in point of constitutional ideas, as widely from the rebellious Democrates of Paris, as it is possible for contrariety of opinion to separate into two distinct forms of Government.

Mad, however, with the spirit of republicanism, and flushed with the victory which democracy had gained over monarchy in France, the friends of that revolution, in this country, entertained some wild idea that there was a probability of setting the people against their Sovereign, and of overturning the Constitution of the Empire.

For this purpose the most inflammatory pamphlets and advertisements have been dispersed throughout every part of Great Britain, and agents employed to ripen the lower order of the people into an open aversion to the present system of government—and to crown the whole it was determined to have public feasts on the 14th of this month in the metropolis, and in the most populous and flourishing towns of the kingdom, as marks of veneration for the approbation of the too successful rebellion in France.

An act so treasonable to the Constitution, and so subversive of the real happiness and welfare of the public, became the subject of general animadversion; and as the great body of the people (some few Dissenting individuals excepted) really loved their King, and in a manner worshipped the laws by which they were governed, it was natural to suppose that some decisive indignation would manifest itself against those factious traitors. And sorry are we to add, that by accounts from Birmingham, received at the Secretary of State's Office on Saturday, and by several private letters it appears, that the loyal spirit of the numerous inhabitants of that great manufacturing town broke

51

forth with the greatest violence, and fell with uncommon fury on those who were celebrating the anniversary of the new fangled Government in France.

A public meeting, it seems, had been announced to commemorate the 14th of July at the Hotel in Temple-row; to which a number of persons, mostly Presbytereans, repaired.

In their way thither, the populace, who met for the purpose, hooted and hissed them incessantly, and from this general mark of disapprobation it was thought the Revolutionists would have retired, and by that prudent step appease the threatening tumult. But obstinate in pursuit of their favourite plan, they persisted, and flattering themselves that the pamphlets, advertisements, and missionaries of the Constitutional Society had made a considerable number of commonwealth proselytes, they set the voice of the people at defiance, and openly braved their threats.

The consequence of this was, that in the evening every window in the Hotel was smashed to pieces, but not before the company, in defence of their lives, had stolen away in the best manner they could. It was in vain that the Magistrates and peace officers attempted to stop the fury of the public—such feeble resistance only served to add vigour to their conduct, and push them forward to greater vengeance. They proceeded from the Hotel to DOCTOR PRIESTLEY's Conventicle, in powerful force; and having first torn down the pulpit they then gutted the building, and setting fire to its furniture made a triumphant bonfire of the whole. Not content, however, with reducing the desks, seats, pews, &c. to ashes, they Bastilled the building, and left not a stone of it unturned.

Whilst this was going forward, a detachment proceeded to the Doctor's dwelling-house at Fairhill which they razed to the ground, burning all his philosophical apparatus, his library and furniture. Fortunately the Doctor had made his escape a few minutes before their arrival, which so incensed the people, who certainly meant to sacrifice him, that they had an effigy made as nearly to resemble his figure as time would permit, and after hanging it up in the most ignominious manner, it was burned to ashes, amidst the shouts and acclamations of near ten thousand people.

The old Meeting House was also burned, and the walls fell in about eleven o'clock, and at that time the new Jerusalem Meeting house it was thought would share the same fate, as well as the private houses of several of the leading Revolution Dinner Men.

It was somewhat remarkable, that Doctor Priestley, who, in public, was the most abstemious man alive, and who was ever preaching against the luxuries of life, and the use of strong liquors, and who, it was thought by the vulgar, lived in a manner upon philosophy, should have had his cellars stored with the choicest liquors, of which numbers of the people when his house was gutted, drank most freely, and many of the lower order, to such excess, that they became quite intoxicated. The Doctor happily contrived to get away his plate, and is himself at a relation's house in a distant part of the country.

One private house belonging to Mr. Ryland, who was at the Dinner, and rather loud in praise of Democracy, has been pulled down. It was the house formerly inhabited by Mr. Baskerville.

During the whole of those transactions, the populace continually shouted "God save the King."—"Long live the King, and the Constitution in Church and State."—"Down with all the abettors of French rebellion."—"Church and King"—"Down with the Rumps"—"No Olivers"—"No false Rights of Man."

To endeavour to appease this tumult, Lord Aylesford, at the head of several hundred respectable persons, marched to Dr. Priestley's house, and prevailed upon the persons assembled there to disperse, and it was thought his Lordship, who is much respected, would be able to stop the universal destruction of the property, and perhaps the lives of those hot-headed mistaken Revolution Society Men.

All was tumult—all was apprehension. There was no knowing where the fury of an enraged multitude might stop.

Such are the first sad effects of Mr. Paine's pamphlet, and the recommendation of the Constitutional Society to the public to read it. It has had the effect that sensible men foresaw—it has raised the avenging arm of the nation, who instead of abiding by the doctrine there laid down, seized the first opportunity to shew their abhorence of the atheistical precepts of the new RIGHTS OF MAN.

Several inflammatory and treasonable hand-bills respecting the glory of the Revolution in France, were distributed on the morning of the 14th in every part of Birmingham; which, instead of gaining the support of the people, had the contrary effect, and produced thousands of enemies without making one friend to the new doctrine of Messrs. Priestley, Paine, and Co. We have all the handbills in our possession, but must forbear to publish them, as it would give them a degree of celebrity they by no means deserve.

Joseph Priestley, a Unitarian minister and a pioneering scientist, was a prominent supporter of the Revolution. His own account of these 'Church and King' riots in Birmingham contradicted The Times: *Priestley insisted that the mob was out to attack Dissenters, and was not primarily hostile to political radicalism. The truth lay somewhere between his account and that of* The Times. *Priestley and his son William were both made honorary French citizens in 1792.*

July 23rd, 1791

On Saturday a number of people assembled in the *Champ de Mars,* to hear the inflammatory speeches of certain violent Republicans; some of whom, *it is pretended,* are Prussians and English. Their number gradually increased, and at noon four commissioners arrived from the Jacobins, bringing with them a petition which they invited the mob to sign, in order that it should be presented to the National Assembly. . .

.   .   .

Two men, one of them an invalid with a wooden leg, and the other a young hair-dresser, having imprudently concealed themselves under the boards which form the ascent to the altar of liberty, with an intention, *as it was said,* to peep at the ladies' legs, through holes which they had bored for that purpose, were discovered, and immediately dragged out of their lurking place.

They were accused of having intended to set fire to the altar of liberty; and it was pretended that on them some tow and matches had been found.

Others said that they had a design to blow up the *Champ de Mars.*

In one moment their heads were off.

Not satisfied with these summary proceedings, the mob were preparing to drag the bodies through the streets; but they were fortunately prevented by the National Guards.

The municipality being of opinion that these proceedings indicated a conspiracy against public order, and the deliberations of the National Assembly, resolved to proceed to the Champ de la Federation; they accordingly put themselves in motion, with the National Guard and the Cavalry, under the orders of the Commander General, followed by five pieces of cannon, and preceded by the Red Flag.

At half an hour past seven, more than two hours after Martial Law had been published at the Hotel de Ville, they arrived at the Champ de la Federation, which the Municipality entered by the hollow path cut into the Amphitheatre. The mob appeared on the two eminences on each side of that path, and calling out, *"Down with the Red Flag, down with the bayonets,"* they held out bludgeons, and threw stones at the Municipality and troops.

The Municipality ordered to fire over their heads; the shower of stones was continued; one of the mob fired a pistol at the Municipality. The National Guard fired; nobody was hurt. The mob returned to the charge; the fire of the National Guard was continued. The Municipality and Commander General endeavoured in vain to put a stop to the attack: it was impossible for them, in consequence of the rapidity of the shock, to make the three proclamations, warning peaceable citizens to depart.

The Municipality entered the Champ de la Federation: the mob fled to the lower part, and there it was that the firing was most incessant. At the moment of the drawing up of the minutes, the Municipality said that they understood, that, on the side of the mob, there had been eleven or twelve killed, and about ten or twelve wounded. On the other side, a trooper was struck from his horse by a stone; some of the National Guards have been wounded; two chasseurs, who were separated from the troop, were killed, and likewise a gunner.

The Champ de la Federation was quickly evacuated. The Commander General rallied the troops, and they returned with the Municipality at ten o'clock, who immediately communicated to the Department an account of their proceedings.

One of the bodies was brought to the *Palais Royal,* and over it one of the Republican incendiaries attempted to make a harangue with a view to encourage the mob to further acts of courage.—But he was soon laid hold of, and his audience dispersed by the National Guards.

The streets have been ever since illuminated at night, and the National Guards, to the amount of 20,000, patrole all the streets of Paris during the whole night. The Palais Royal had been kept shut at night, and the mob is entirely excluded.

The enemies of the Revolution are accused of having been the principal cause of this tumult. Among these are reckoned Messrs. Roberspierre, Pethion, Gregoire, and Anthoine.

55

The 'Massacre of the Champ de Mars', and the repression which followed, brought a severe but temporary check to the forces of radical Jacobinism. The Times confused its dates. The first petition mentioned here, demanding the abdication of the king, was signed on the Saturday, but it was not welcomed with enthusiasm. On Sunday, the radical Jacobins rapidly collected more than six thousand signatures for another petition demanding the King's trial and replacement 'by a new executive power'. It was on Sunday that the two men were discovered under the altar, and that the massacre took place.

January 4th, 1792

FRANCE

PARIS, *Dec. 30, 1791*

The riot which has taken place at the *Feuillans* Club is of too serious a nature to be passed over in silence.

The Club which used to be held at the Feuillans is entirely hostile to the turbulent and republican Jacobins, and is composed of men of the first abilities and experience, and known to be staunch friends to true monarchy and to genuine liberty.

Two hundred and sixty-four Members of the present Assembly belong to it, besides eight hundred citizens, many of whom were the most distinguished Members of the Constituent Assembly such as *Messrs. D'André, Barnave,* the *Lameths, Duport, Rabaud, Thouret, &c. &c. &c.*

On the 21st inst. the club was attacked by a number of men, armed with clubs, who forced their way into the Hall at the Feuillans. There they were guilty of the most criminal excesses. They insulted the Members;—they would permit no kinds of discussions, and they openly declared that they came there on purpose to demolish the Assembly.

M. CHARON, the President, sent to the Mayor, desiring that a Commissioner of Police might attend to keep the peace. The Mayor refused to send a Commissioner, but said that he would take every precaution in his power. The Mayor was informed that, on the 23rd, there was a probability of another riot. The Mayor ordered then the Commissioner of Police to attend, and to have force in readiness, if it should be necessary. The riot accordingly took place. Both parties came armed, and dared each other to combat. It was solely owing to M. *Prestat,* a municipal officer, that a general massacre did not take place.

The Members of the Club were the first to pay due obedience to the Law by quitting the Hall. The rioters insisted on the dissolution of the Club. They were treated with contempt. M. *Merlin* then denounced to the National Assembly an officer of the National Guards, as has already been mentioned in the papers. To avoid all occasions of future riots, the club agreed to change their place of meeting.

M. *Petion's* conduct on this occasion seeems to have been exceedingly partial. He says in a letter which he wrote to the President, that probably, there might be in the club, men who are lovers of order, and friends to the Constitution, but that he believed many of them were hostile to the constitution and promoters of tumults.

The hatred betweeen this Club and the Jacobins is at its height, and will divide the whole kingdom into two parties, inveterate against each other, which will be productive of the most terrible consequences, although in its progress it must tend to assist the cause of the French Princes.

The taxes not being received, the former property of the Clergy pays for all, though intended merely to acquit the national debt; for the last month the deficiency amounts to eighteen millions of livres.

The *Jacobins* are going to establish an English news-paper, in which their transactions will appear; it is to be distributed *gratis* among the clubs of Great Britain; but the grand object in view is to disseminate their principles among *Irishmen,* whom they think ripe for what La Fayette called *"le plus saint des devoirs."*

The Feuillants Club was a right-wing breakaway from the Jacobins Club, after the Massacre of the Champ de Mars. The fight The Times *describes above, though of little account in itself, shows how rapidly the political situation was now polarizing: the constitutionalists were suspected of preparing a military putsch, through the Feuillants and the army command under Lafayette, to restore the powers of the monarchy and the privileges of nobility. Of the men mentioned, Barnave, Duport, one of the Lameth brothers and d'André were in secret correspondence with the King and Queen, urging them to accept the constitution as a means of slowly regaining political authority.*

On April 20th, 1792 France declared war on Austria. The forces of the emigration along the eastern border were a threat to the Revolution and Louis hoped, by consenting to wage a phoney war ('politique et d'observation'), to improve his popularity. The driving force in the campaign for war was the group in the Jacobin Club round Brissot, which hoped not only to destroy the émigrés by a direct offensive against their headquarters at Koblenz but to involve the King irrevocably in the fortunes of the Revolution and end his suspected links with his own brothers abroad. Narbonne, Louis's new war minister, perceived war as a way of restoring the monarchy's reputation and enhancing his own. The only effective opposition to war came from the Jacobin faction led by Robespierre, who argued that the Revolution within France must be completed before any attack on counter-revolution abroad could be launched. Out of the break between Brissot and Robespierre over the war developed the great division within the revolutionary leadership between the 'Montagne', the radical Jacobins, and the loose coalition of more moderate groups known — inaccurately — as the 'Girondins'.

April 24th, 1792

DECLARATION OF WAR, BY THE KING OF THE FRENCH AGAINST THE KING OF HUNGARY[1]

The news of the intended war on the part of France against the King of Hungary and Bohemia, was announced in *The Times* of Monday se'n-night, and the event has verified our intelligence. Lord GOWER's[2] courier arrived yesterday from Paris, which place he left on Friday evening last, and brings the following information:

On Friday morning last the King of FRANCE went to the National Assembly, and proposed to DECLARE WAR AGAINST THE KING OF HUNGARY AND BOHEMIA. When the Courier came away, war was not formally declared,—but Lord Gower says, that it certainly would be before his messenger reached London,—and that an insurrection was expected in Paris.

It is easy to perceive, that this declaration of hostilities is

[1] The 'King of Hungary and Bohemia' was the Austrian Emperor.
[2] Lord Gower had succeeded the Duke of Dorset as British Ambassador.

58

solely the advice of the JACOBIN Ministry, who are so impatient for attacking the King of Hungary, that they will not brook the delay of their new minister to Vienna's interposing his offices to prevent the expediency of such calamity. The plan of the French is, to enter Flanders and Brabant without delay, in the hopes of fomenting an insurrection in those Countries, and distressing the King of Hucgary. At the same time it is intended to make a diversion into the King's territories by the way of Strasburgh.

The dismissal of the King's personal guard force by the National Assembly (May 29th), and popular fears that the dominant 'Brissotins' were trying to usurp the control of Paris over the National Guard sections, led to a complex crisis. The government collapsed, ending the attempt at constitutional power-sharing between the monarchy and the revolutionary leadership. On June 20th, rebellious sections of the National Guard invaded the National Assembly and then broke into the palace of the Tuileries. The loyal National Guards referred to in the first paragraph here, who were supposedly protecting the palace, came from the royalist district of Filles de St.-Thomas.

June 26th, 1792

. . . The door of the Palace was shut. The mob threaten to break it open. Some Municipal Officers order it to be opened. The National Guards not having orders, remain inactive; they were without commanders, and grieved to the soul to see the dreadful proceedings, and shocked to think what a scene was going to be acted in the Palace.

In less than five minutes the Monarch's apartments are filled with 20,000 men, armed with pikes, with blades of knives, with saws, &c. &c. dragging after them cannons into the interior parts of the Palace.

The KING placed himself in a window in the midst of four National Guards. The brave Acloque stood before his Majesty, and shielded him with his body.

The cries, the howlings which resounded all round him were sufficient to appal the stoutest heart. Every flag unfurled before him, had inscriptions intended to make him tremble. On one of them were these words "Tremble tyrants; the citizens are under arms." On another—"Union of the Fauxbourgs St.

59

Antoine and St. Marceau."—On a third—"Behold the Sans-Culottes".[1]

Messrs *Dossouville, Dorival,* and *Auger,* Officers of Peace, ran to the Assembly to inform the Legislators of the dangers with which the King was surrounded.—The Assembly adjourned instantly.

Meanwhile the KING was presented with a cap on the top of a pike. His Majesty took it and put it on his head; ribbands were offered to him on the end of another pike. These also he accepted. The crowd began to press upon him.—A National Guard was nearly forced out of his place, near his Majesty;—"The King" cried this brave fellow, "is our safeguard, I would not desert him for a hundred thousand Crowns!"—A Municipal officer attempted to speak, but could not be heard. Several Members made the same attempt, without success.

M. *Santerre*[2] then tried what he could do.—A roar ensued of—"Long live Petion![3] Long live the good, the worthy Petion!"—The good, the worthy Petion then addressed the King.—"The people," says he, "have appeared with dignity, and with dignity they will depart. Your Majesty may make yourself perfectly easy." *Santerre* orders the Deputation to come forward.

The spokesman accordingly demanded that the patriotic Ministers be re-instated. That the *Veto* be retracted, relative to the two obnoxious decrees.

The King answered:

"I have sworn to maintain the Constitution, and I will defend it at the risk of my life."

The QUEEN was then in the Council Chamber, having on her left hand the *Prince Royal,* and on her right *Madame Royale,* and Madame *Lamballe.*

Santerre desired the Guards who stood before the QUEEN to get out of the way. She was then offered a red cap, which she received, and put it on the Prince's head. She then took a cockade off the hat of one of the National Guards, and stuck it on the Prince's cap.

Clamours were renewed of "Long live the nation! Long live the *Sans-Culottes!* Long live liberty! No veto!"

---

[1] 'Sans-culottes' originally denoted those who wore ordinary trousers, as opposed to those who wore breeches.

[2] Santerre was the Commander of National Guard.

[3] Pétion was the Mayor of Paris.

The eyes of the leaders of the mob, and of many of the mob themselves glistened with rage. "Long live *Santerre!*" A grenadier attempting to quiet them, the Prince told him, "Let them alone, my friend,—let their words be ever so injurious it is all the same to me."

This scene lasted till eight o'clock. The Justices of the Peace tried all they could to prevail on the mob to retire, but all in vain; M. *Santerre,* however, their ringleader, was more persuasive, and the mob at length withdrew.

During the whole of this extraordinary scene, the KING never betrayed the least fear, nor seemed in the least alarmed. He appeared cool, collected, full of dignity, and the truly great man. Oppressed with heat, he desired some water to drink. A bottle was given him, and he drank without hesitation, without even seeming to suspect that there was any danger in this, and that he was performing an act of intrepidity. The events of this day have for ever disgraced France in the eyes of mankind!

The left of the Jacobin Club, co-operating with the revolutionary sections of Paris, now began to prepare an insurrection to remove the King and force the summoning of a National Convention. Opinion against the King was hardened by the 'Manifesto' of the Duke of Brunswick, published on August 1st, which threatened Paris with complete destruction if Louis were harmed and committed the émigrés and their foreign allies to total counter-revolution. Two days later, 47 out of 48 Paris sections petitioned for the removal of the King and the summoning of a Convention. The insurrection took place on August 10th.

August 16th, 1792

FRANCE

PARIS, —Saturday at Noon.

IRRUPTION INTO THE PALACE DES TUILLERIES—BATTLE BETWEEN THE SWISS GUARDS AND THE SANS CULOTTES*—ESCAPE OF THE KING AND ROYAL FAMILY OUT OF THE HANDS OF THE REGICIDES—MASSACRE OF THE SWISS GUARDS—THE PALACE OF THE

*A party of the mob so called

61

August 16th, 1792

TUILLERIES PLUNDERED, AND THE ADJACENT BUILDINGS SET ON FIRE—THE KING AND ROYAL FAMILY SAFE.

(From our regular Correspondent.)

I now sit down to write you a full and distinct account of the most tragical event that ever my eyes witnessed. It is such as makes humanity shudder, and my blood freezes with horror at the very recollection of the massacre and distress to which I was an unwilling spectator. It is with very heartfelt grief that I am obliged to recount to you a scene of bloodshed which will ever remain as a stain on the history of my country, for the outrages were not provoked by any perfidy or stratagem on the part of the Royal Family, but were the result of cool, deliberate, and premeditated revenge.

The event which has just taken place will hardly be believed by posterity. More than a week ago it was everywhere foretold by the numerous incendiaries who are the main springs of the various groupes of the Palais Royal, of the Terrace des Feuillans, &c. They had repeatedly declared that it was resolved to massacre the Swiss Guards,—to drive out of the Tuilleries those National Guards who had remained faithful to the King,—and to destroy the Palace, that it might be no longer the abode of Kings. All these particulars were too unfortunately put in execution on Friday. Although all the inhabitants of Paris were fully informed of the dreadful catastrophe which was to take place; although the day *and the hour* had been fixed upon and known; although the banditti had declared that exactly at midnight on Thursday the *generale* would begin to beat, and the alarm-bells ring;—yet the Parisians were so infatuated, and in such a state of consternation, that they seemed quietly to bow their necks, and to prepare to be butchered without resistance, if it should be the supreme will of the Mob that they should.

The preparations that were making on Thursday evening threatened some terrible explosion. The streets were illuminated, and the crouds of people in them greater than was ever remembered. It is evident that the decision of the Assembly on the affair of *M. de la Fayette*[1] had greatly enraged the Jacobin mob,

---

[1] On August 8th the Assembly had rejected the motion for the impeachment of Lafayette, who had deserted his post as army commander, after vainly trying to suppress the Jacobins and halt the popular attacks on the Royal Family.

and during the whole day their adherents were busy in exciting such a clamour as might ensure them success on the question for deposing the King.

Scarcely had the clock struck twelve on Thursday night, when all the bells of Paris began to ring the alarm, and the *generale* was beat in every quarter of the capital. In the Fauxbourgs and in some other places the armed mobs were a long time in collecting together. While the *Sans Culottes* were assembling in the extremities of the town, the National Guards were joining their respective battalions. Some of them went to the Palace, where already near 600 Swiss had assembled. The remainder of the night was thus passed in the greatest confusion, to the great consternation of the Parisians. The *Sans Culottes,* joined by a great number of National Guards, did not arrive in force at the Palace, till between six and seven o'clock in the morning of yesterday.

At eight o'clock in the morning a patrole of Swiss Guards was attacked in the *Champs Elysées.* This patrole was moving towards the castle, and also some courtiers, and some of the King's guards. An alarm was spread, and numbers of armed citizens of the battalion of Marseilles, and of Federates from the different Departments, began to fill the avenues to the Palace and the National Assembly, demanding vengeance on those traitors whom they had seized.—A scene of terrible confusion ensued: The unfortunate victims underwent a sort of mock trial, were convicted, and execution immediately followed. Six of the soldiers had their heads instantly struck off their shoulders, and the mob sat in judgment on the rest, as if they had been coolly guided by real principles of justice, although the sentence was already sealed with blood. It does not appear that there was any ground of accusation against these men, except that there was found on them several cases of pistols loaded. This was a sufficient ground of suspicion, and they were accordingly hung up in the *Place de Vendome,* and their heads afterwards carried about the town on pikes.

The attack at the Palace began before ten o'clock. It was conducted by a regiment of Cordeliers, some Federates of Marseilles, the Federates of Brest, and a battalion of Guards from the quarter of St. Antoine. A Marseillois Officer appeared at the principal door of the Palace, and demanded entrance for himself and his banditti, from a Swiss officer who commanded there. The Swiss replied that his orders would not permit him to comply. The Marseillois officer instantly applied a pistol to his breast and shot him through the heart. That moment the carnage began, and it lasted the whole day.

During this time, the inhabitants of all the Fauxbourgs were repairing to the *Palace* and to the *National Assembly,* accompanied by all the Sections of Paris, armed in the same manner as they were on the 20th of June, and calling out for the dethronement of the King—that he was a Traitor, and had forfeited the Crown. The KING perceiving such a mob of banditti, with fury in their looks began to be alarmed. Just at that moment, he received a message from the *Directors of the Department of Paris,* warning him of his danger, and advising him to go immediately to the National Assembly, and to take his family with him. He was scarcely out of the Palace before the mob, collected together on the *Place du Carousel,* insisted on being admitted immediately into the Courts of the Palace. It was impossible for the guards to prevent their irruption. Having rushed in, in vast numbers, they took possession of the cannons which they found in the Courts, and which had been abandoned by the gunners, who had joined the insurgents.

It was observed, that these banditti, as well as the guards themselves, were not headed by any officers; but the mob cried out, that they could do without them, for their officers could not be trusted.

During this attempt to break into the Palace, a very heavy fire was kept up on both sides, and a great many persons killed. Cannons were pointed to prevent the entrance into the Palace, but the numbers and strength of the mob rendered resistance ineffectual, and they at length penetrated into the interior parts of it. The first resistance within was from the top of the grand staircase, where the Swiss made a very firm stand, but the mob unawed, and encouraged by the cry of Liberty, Victory, or Death, soon made their way up the staircase, when the Swiss gave way, and a general massacre ensued. They had defended themselves with great intrepidity, and slain numbers of their assassins, but being attacked at the same instant by the National Guards within, posted there to protect the King, and by the armed banditti below, they were between two fires, and the slaughter was of course great. The Swiss Guards had been weakened by their having sent a detachment of their corps to join some National Guards who protected the King on his way to the National Assembly, and when the King was arrived there, most of those guards dispersed to go to breakfast.

The massacre was greater than can hardly be credited, and it is reported with great authority, and the report is confirmed by both parties, that 1500 persons, including women and children, were slain or wounded during this day. There was not one Swiss soldier spared.[1] About 60 who were not killed on the spot, were taken prisoners and conducted to the Town Hall of the Commons of Paris. It was intended that they should have here a summary trial, but the women, particularly the *Poissardes*, rushed in torrents into the Hall, crying for vengeance, and the Swiss Guards were then given up to their fury, and every man of them murdered on the spot. Among the Swiss officers and others killed, we find the names of M. *d'Affri*, Colonel; M. *Mandat*, the Commandant; M. *Erlac*, M. *Carle*, the Jeweller, &c. &c.

M. *Sulau*, the QUEEN's Secretary, is likewise among those whose heads were cut off in the Palace.

A scene equally shocking took place in another part of the town, in the *Rue St. Honoré*, where an action took place between another party of the Swiss and some of the Federates and Guards. The slaughter was here very considerable, particularly among the Brest Federates, who being mistaken by the National Guards for Swiss soldiers, from their wearing a red uniform, were fired upon by their own party and many killed.—The Swiss barracks were in the course of the day set fire to and burnt down.

Many of the women belonging to the Palace, and some others met an equally unfortunate fate. They had fled for safety and had reached the bridge, when they were pursued by the mob. Knowing that their lives were in danger if they were taken, about 20 threw themselves over the ballustrades into the water and were drowned.

The Palace of the Thuilleries is almost wholly destroyed, all the doors and windows of it being broken to pieces. The mob not contented with having murdered all those within it, afterwards placed cannon loaded with ball and pointed against it, by which means several of the walls are beaten down. The furniture was thrown out of the windows and destroyed; and all the adjacent buildings are in flames. In the evening the Statue on the *Place*

[1] In fact about three hundred of the nine hundred guards survived.

Vendome was thrown down, and the mob have likewise destroyed that on the *Place de Louis* XV.

M. *Santerre*, leader of the *Sans Culottes*, is appointed—by whom we know not—Commandant General of the National Guards. M. *Petion* continues to be Mayor, and M. *Manuel* Procureur Syndic of the Commons.

Nothing was heard yesterday but the noise of cannon and musquetry.

During all these disorders, the King and the Royal Family were sitting among the Deputies of the National Assembly where they had taken refuge. There the King heard pronounced the decree, which deprives him of all his functions, of every atom of power,—which cashiers his Ministers, annihilates the Civil List, and convokes the primary Assemblies in order to appoint Deputies to a National Convention. . . .

The Times correspondent, evidently a Frenchman, now gave vent to all his pent-up royalism. But he was right in his estimate that the great Insurrectionary Commune which struck on August 10th had changed utterly the pace and form of the Revolution. The long 'limited monarchy' preludes were over: the central phase of the Revolution had begun.

August 17th, 1792

"Since my last, events have succeeded each other with such rapidity, that I can only give you an account of a few out of the many, which equally demand attention.

"The KING and his whole Family are still in the National Assembly, in a state of arrest. He is to be removed to the *Hotel de la Chancelleries, Place Vendome,* where he is to be allowed guards for the safety of his person. He is to have 500,000 livres for his subsistence, and that of the Royal Family. He is not to be allowed to write a single letter, nor to receive any. His very domestics are to be appointed by M. PETION.—To this condition is the KING of FRANCE reduced. He will, from his apartments, see the statue of LOUIS XVI. in fragments on the ground. Those of LOUIS XV. LOUIS XIII. and HENRY IV. have shared the same fate. Even the wooden statue of PHILIP THE FAIR in the Church *de Notre Dame* is destroyed.

"While war is thus carrying on against the effigies of our Kings, and against their living descendant,—the Commons are employed in laying the foundation of a new Constitution. Already the National Assembly have absolved themselves of the oath which they took formerly, to be faithful to the Constitution. The fashionable oath is now "I swear to maintain liberty and equality with all my might, and to die in defence of them.""

"This is the principle on which the new Constitution is to be established. It leads directly to an equal division of property, and to Agrarian laws. The Commons are in full possession of all power and authority. They have conferred on the Sections the right of judging every Citizen who shall be denounced, and to pass on him what sentence they please. They have erected a provisionary Tribunal, to which they refer every man sent to them as a criminal, who is summarily judged, and instantly executed. Every moment, fresh victims fall under the sword of this new Tribunal. Every person is positively prevented from leaving Paris. All those who are possessed of property are in a general consternation. Ecclesiastics are particularly ferreted out and imprisoned. The Nobility share the same fate. PRINCE DE ROHAN CHABOT was arrested yesterday and will, no doubt, be soon sacrificed. ABBE DILLON, of an Irish Family, has been massacred in his own house. Yesterday, Twelve Ecclesiastics were arrested who had taken refuge in the Irish College. Persecution is, in short, at its height.

"To give you some idea of the principles by which our present rulers are actuated, take the following anecdote:

"Yesterday, *à la Commune,* a motion was made to send 6000 men to Orleans to put to death all the prisoners confined there as state criminals. This motion was honored with the most unbounded applause, and it is not doubted but it will be speedily put in execution.

(We learn late last night, that all the state prisoners at Orleans have been murdered.)

"The preparations are making for speedily forming camps round Paris. Cannons are already placed on *la butte Monmartre.* Another Camp is to be formed *à l'Ecole Militaire.* No news from the armies. All letters are intercepted. Most of our Journals, all those at least which are unfavorable to the new cause are suppressed. The City continues to be illuminated every night.

"Every stratagem has been employed to excite the fury of

the rabble against the Royal Family, and to bring them to the scaffold. For this purpose, not only hand bills are in daily circulation, but the licentious editors of the Jacobin Journals invent the most gross calumnies; which they know must remain uncontradicted, as the Gazettes in the opposite interest have been prohibited to be published. In one of these papers of yesterday, written by the execrable Gorsas, a letter is published, which he says was found in the QUEEN's writing-desk at the time the Palace was pillaged, from her Majesty to the Austrian Minister at Brussels, recommending a long list of proscribed friends to the royal cause to his particular favor. She is therein made to write—how much they are entitled to his protection from the services they have done her and the King, and that she hopes the time draws nigh, when she shall be able to reward all her friends;—that she looks forward with a pleasing hope to the time when the DUKE OF BRUNSWICK enters Paris.—By this and other means are the populace blindly urged on to their own ultimate destruction, while those who invent these atrocious calumnies are extolled as good citizens and patriots."

The deputies suggested the King's confinement in the Ministry of Justice, Place Vendôme, but the Commune—the city's insurrectionary government—insisted on the security of the keep of the 'Temple'.

August 17th, 1792

ADDRESS FROM THE GUNNERS OF THE BATTALION DE ST. MERY, TO THE NATIONAL ASSEMBLY

"*Representatives of the People,*
"Having escaped death, the Gunners of the Battalion de St. Mery think proper to declare to you solemnly, that going this morning (August 10), to the Thuilleries, with an intention to defend, with their brazen-mouths, the first public *Functionnaire,* they did not make use of their artillery till they were most furiously fired upon by a horde of Satellites, who assassinated them from those very windows from whence a fanatical King fired himself on his people.
"*Legislators!* This day is the most glorious of our whole

68

lives, since we have exposed them for the public safety.

"*Representatives of the People,*

"Your moments are sacred. Your business is to save the Empire. For us let it suffice that we swear, in the sanctuary of the laws, that we are, every instant, ready on the first signal, to perish for the safety of your persons, for the maintenance of your decrees, and for the extermination of all internal and external Counter-revolutionists".....

September 5th, 1792

FRANCE

At length we have received a letter from our *regular Correspondent* at Paris, after a suspension of nearly *three weeks.* We had great reason to dread from his silence that he might be among the many who have lost their lives within the last three weeks, or more probably among those who have been taken up on groundless suspicion. His letter is very short, and as follows:

PARIS—THURSDAY, AUGUST 30.

"You say truly, that you are fearful none of your letters have reached me; but I am not surprized at it, for all the correspondence of the kingdom has been stopped and searched during the last fortnight. It begins however to be resumed, and your letter of the 25th has regularly come to hand, without having been apparently opened. Let us hope that this crisis will soon see its end, and that we may again have the liberty of speaking our sentiments freely on every subject.

"I am glad to find that you are not ignorant of the most important occurrences that have happened since I last wrote to you. The licentious patriotism of this metropolis has ruined France, has stained the national honour, and in short destroyed the press, the types, and all the implements of printing in those houses which were supposed to be inimical to the events of the 10th of August. Not a printing-office has been spared. What scenes of horror and devastation could I relate to you on this and other subjects, did not prudence interdict the communication. After saying thus much, you cannot be surprized at my not

69

complying with the request you make me. But have patience and rely that I will not lose a favourable moment to resume my correspondence, which you mention in such flattering terms, when I can do it with safety. I trust that this period is not far distant."

In the Postscript he says—"At the instant of my closing this letter, the people are entering my house armed to search it. I suppose it is in search of fire arms.—Adieu."

The Prussians crossed the frontier in August. On September 2nd, Paris heard that Verdun was besieged (it had actually fallen on the 1st). Georges Danton, Minister of Justice but effective leader of the defence of the Revolution, was among those who now issued emergency proclamations. The committee in charge of prisons and security, which failed to prevent the massacre of 'internal enemies', included Jean-Paul Marat.

September 8th, 1792

. . . "In consequence of these resolutions, the *tocsin* was rung, the alarm guns were fired, and the people soon assembled in very great numbers in the *Champ de Mars.* The Municipal officers on horseback, and in their scarfs, proclaimed in every quarter of the town, that *the country was in danger,* and that it became all good citizens to fly to its relief. The people answered with loud huzzas, crying out, *'Long live the Nation, Liberty, Equality; down with all Tyrants.'* Their minds were further inflamed by a report that was industriously circulated, that the people were betrayed.

"The mob proclaimed in answer to the Municipal Officers, that they had no objection to fly to the frontiers to beat the foreign enemy, and they wished no better sport, but first they *would purge the nation of its internal enemies.* It was proposed to go to the prisons of the *Abbey,* where those accused of high treason were principally confined, and to the *Carmes,* where the refractory priests were imprisoned. This idea seemed to be highly relished, and in consequence, hordes of banditti flocked to these places, and demanded a list of the names of the persons confined, and the nature of their crimes.

"The National Assembly when they heard of what was passing without doors, sent a deputation of twelve Members to

70

persuade the mob to desist. But it was all in vain—the massacre had begun, and their voices were drowned amidst the shouts of the rabble. Not a single person accused of high treason or theft, nor a priest that was found, escaped this horrible slaughter. They were all butchered in cold blood, and M. de MONTMORIN (whose fate I expected) though he had been acquitted by a Jury, was killed between the legs of one of the deputies, in attempting to escape.

"Among other principal personages who fell victims in this slaughter, I hear, is the Princess de LAMBALLE, Madame de TOURZELLES, and some other Ladies in the suite of the Queen, confined in the gaol *de la Force*. All those prisoners confined for debt, or trivial offences, were screened from the rage of the populace, and a great number of them was permitted to escape.

"An aged officer of the King's former body guard, some priests, and a reverend Bishop of the old School, were about the same [time] taken up on suspicion near the Palace. They were about to be conducted to the Municipality, but on their way, the mob chose to take the law into their own hands, and hanged them *à la lanterne*. I have heard of many more executions of a similar nature, though I cannot sufficiently particularize them.

September 10th, 1792

The following report of the massacre on Sunday, has been made by a Member of the National Assembly. Although we know that this report does not state the whole of the facts, which for obvious reasons are concealed, it is however, a very proper article to be here inserted; but it is to be remarked, that this report relates to the *prisons only*.

"The Commission assembled during the suspension of the night sitting, being informed by several citizens, that the people were continuing to rush in great numbers towards the different prisons, and were there exercising their vengeance, thought it necessary to write to the Council General of the Community, to learn officially the true state of things. The Community sent back word, that they had ordered a deputation to render an account to the commission of what had happened. At two o'clock the deputation, consisting of Mess. Tallion, Tronchon, and Cuirate, was introduced into the hall of the Assembly. M.

71

September 10th, 1792

Tronchon then said, that the greater part of the prisons were empty; that about four hundred prisoners were massacred; that he had thought it prudent to release all prisoners confined for debt at the prison *La Force,* and that he had done the same thing at *Saint Pelagie.* That when he returned to the Community, he recollected that he had neglected to visit that part at *La Force,* where the women were confined; that he immediately returned, and set at liberty twenty-four. That he and his colleague had taken under their particular protection Madame *Tourzelle,* and Madame *Saint Brice,* and that they had conducted these two ladies to the Section of the *Rights of Man,* to be kept there till they are tried.

"M. *Tallien* added, that when he went to the Abbaye, the people were demanding the registers from the keeper; that the prisoners confined on account of crimes imputed to them on the 10th of August, and those confined for forging assignats, were almost all butchered, and that only eleven of them were saved. The Council of the Community had dispatched a deputation to endeavour to check the brutal fury of the mob: their Solicitor first addressed them, and employed every means to appease them. His efforts, however, were attended with no success, and multitudes around him fell victims to the barbarity of the populace.

"The mob next proceeded to the *Chatelet,* where they likewise sacrificed all the prisoners. About midnight they were collected round *la Force,* to which the Commissioners instantly repaired, but were not able to prevail on the people to desist from their sanguinary proceedings. Several Deputations were successively sent to try if they could restore tranquility, and orders were given to the Commandant General to draw out detachments of the National Guards; but as the service of the barriers required such a great number of men, a sufficiency was not left to repress the audacity of the populace. The Commissioners once more attempted to bring back the ungovernable and infatuated multitude to a sense of justice and humanity; but they could not make the least impression on their minds, or check their ferocity or vengeance.

"M. *Guiraud,* the third Commissioner, said—'We proceeded to the Bicetre with seven pieces of cannon. The people, though they exercised their vengeance, rendered justice, however, to debtors; many of them were released amidst the clashing of

72

arms and shouts of *Vive la Nation*.'—The prisons of the Palais (he added) were all empty, and that very few of those confined in them had escaped death."

"M. Guiraud mentioned that the people were searching the bodies at the *Pont Neuf*, and collecting their money and pocket-books. He added, that he forgot to mention one fact—"In the different prisons, the mob formed a tribunal consisting of twelve persons; after examining the jailor's book, and asking different questions, the judges placed their hands upon the head of the prisoner, and said, 'Do you think that in our consciences we can release this gentleman?'—This word *release* was his condemnation. When they answered *yes*, the accused person, apparently set at liberty, was immediately dashed upon the pikes of the surrounding people. If they were judged innocent, they were released amidst the shouts of *Vive la Nation!*"

(Read this ye ENGLISHMEN, with attention, and ardently pray that your happy Constitution may never be outraged by the despotic tyranny of Equalization.)

September 11th, 1792

PARIS—FRIDAY MORNING, SEPT. 7

"At three o'clock in the afternoon of the fatal 2nd of September, the sanguinary mob reached the *Temple*, where they were met by two of the Commissioners from the National Assembly. It was with great difficulty they could be restrained from further acts of violence; they demanded the head of the QUEEN; the Commissioners therefore to prevent a greater mischief, found it necessary to accompany them to the tower of the *Temple*, one of their leaders carrying on a pole the head of the Princess DE LAMBALLE.

"The Commissioners, attended by an officer of the National Guard, and M. *Palloi*, the manager of the works, round the *Temple*, undertook to inform the KING and QUEEN of what was transacting, and that the people insisted on their viewing the spectacle they had brought. The head of the unfortunate victim was displayed on THEIR MAJESTIES presenting themselves at a window. The QUEEN, and her daughter Madame ELIZABETH, according to the report of a *violent Paris print*, displayed, for the first time, some sensibility; and the KING, who obeyed without

73

any hesitation, said to one of the Commissioners,—*Sir, you are in the right.*

(We have noticed this remark, in order to shew the base calumnies that are propagated concerning these August Personages.)

"The late calamities of this metropolis are given out to have arisen from the deposition of a prisoner confined in the *Hotel la Force,* who attested that assignats of *five livres* each were distributed to the prisoners, by a Magistrate, also in confinement, and that it was told them that in two or three days they were to be set free and to be armed. This is the pretext made use of by *Gorsas* and other Journalists, and on this simple declaration they attempt to justify the massacre. This is however too thin a veil to cover such enormities; at the same time it remains hitherto a profound secret, to whom or to what particular set of people these horrors are to be attributed; for the plan was certainly well laid some days before it was attempted to be put in execution. It is supposed that *Roberspierre,* who is just returned a Deputy for the city, had a principal share in it.

"The workmen are at this time repairing in great numbers to their labours at the encampment without the walls; and battalions are raising in every quarter of the metropolis.

"Yesterday the parish of Neuilly repaired to assist at the works. They were preceded by 200 children, provided with shovels and pick-axes, who made an offering to serve their country. The mothers and sisters followed them, carrying branches of trees. The women are to be employed in making tents, knapsacks, gaiters, &c. On one of the standards carried by the children was the following inscription,— *"Oh, if we had but the strength!"*

The 'Septembrisades' may have cost thirteen hundred lives, two-thirds of them ordinary offenders without political connections. The Times, *its hopes for a moderate Revolution long turned to total opposition, embroidered these terrible days with fictional atrocities whose sadism—the roasting alive of the naked daughters of noblemen, for example—no doubt assisted circulation.*

CHARACTERS OF
FRENCH STATESMEN AND GENERALS.

THE CORDELIER DANTON,
LORD CHANCELLOR OF FRANCE!

From a knowledge of the characters and abilities of the architects, we may form a very perfect idea of the superstructure, which is raising in France,—if the GOTHS do not destroy the foundation.

M. DANTON, celebrated in clubs, and distinguished among the mob, having the honour of being elected a Member of the approaching Convention, claims our attention. His father was a *butcher*—(the son has refined on, and greatly improved the profession!) and amassed, by his industry, sufficient fortune to enable his son to pursue the study of physic. At the recommendation of the late unfortunate Princess of LAMBALLE, he was appointed *Medecin Extraordinaire des Ecuries du Comte* D'ARTOIS. He was—in common with the chiefs of the present mob government, and the libellers of the French Princes,—a parasite; having owed his livelihood and existence to their liberality and countenance. His own medical talents would not have raised his name to its present celebrity; for many of his patients died under his hands; so that, when a page or domestic incurred the displeasure of the Comte D'ARTOIS, he used to threaten to put them under the care of Danton.

He paid his courtship to his master with the most degrading servility, caressing and kissing the horses, because he said he knew them to be favourites with the Comte; and never, until the 14th of July, 1789, did he hear his name pronounced, without taking his hat off. These were facts so well known, as to have been proverbial at Versailles.

Possessed of these courteous qualities, we are not surprised to find him abandon his master when he could no longer serve him, and transfer his courtship to the triumphing mob. He resided in the section *des Cordeliers,* (according to the new geography section *de Marseilles,*) among whose inhabitants, particularly distinguished for their ignorance and rudeness, he became eminent for the vehemence and sedition of his speeches.

75

September 25th, 1792

He is possessed of a very fine natural voice, which commands attention: his speeches are always agreeable to the rabble, as he flatters their passions by inveighing against the Nobility, and exciting them to plunder the opulent. When any Member of the Constituent Assembly used to pronounce, with a fine voice, harangues destitute of oratory or logic, MIRABEAU was accustomed to cry out—*l'eloquence du* DANTON!

In all the popular tumults, which have for these last four years disgraced Paris, DANTON was foremost in animating the people, and pushing them on to crimes. In October, 1789, the *Hotel de Castries,* the *Champ de Mars*—the theatre of his exertions in July last,—bear testimony to his zeal and activity: his services have been rewarded by being frequently called to the chair in the *Club des Cordeliers,*—a club equal to that of the Jacobins for the rebellious dispositions of its Members, but below it in point of art and abilities.

We may judge of its eloquence and principles, from his own speech to the mob in the Champ de Mars. "We are—says he, twenty-five millions of Frenchmen; consequently we have fifty millions of hands armed with swords and poignards: let us send six millions of men to Germany; three millions to Italy and Spain; three millions to Russia and the north of EKUROPE. But beforehand,—in order to get money to pay our brothers and sisters going abroad,—let us send four millions of men to England, to take possession of the Bank of London! The nine millions remaining, are sufficient to cultivate the country,—to destroy LOUIS XVI. and his family, with the National Assembly, and all constituted authorities as aristocrats. Let us do this, and, in a year, all Europe will acknowledge the sovereignty of the French nation. As to new laws, the French people know how to govern without them; and if occasion should present itself that laws should be wanted, let the people make them for every different occasion."

For this speech, he was *decreté*'d *de prise a Corps,* and was obliged to remain concealed until the amnesty, which took place at the King's acceptation of the constitution last year, in the month of September.

This is the man, who is to be one of the judges of his Sovereign, and is a Legislator of his country.—Unhappy King! unhappy Country!

September 26th, 1792

FRANCE

PARIS, SEPT. 21.—*Friday Afternoon*

On the 20th inst. the NATIONAL CONVENTION assembled, for the first time, in the Hall of the Thuilleries, destined for its reception. It consisted of about 400 Deputies, 271 of whom on this occasion, verified their powers. This number exceeding that which had been decreed sufficient to enable the Convention to proceed on its deliberations, it declared itself constituted. During the above sitting M. PETION, who, before he appeared amongst the Conventionalists in quality of Deputy, had given in his resignation as Mayor of Paris, by a letter addressed to the National Assembly, was unanimously elected President.

The Convention instantly sent a deputation to the National Assembly, to announce its organization, and that on that day or the ensuing one it would take possession of the *Salle de Menage*.

The verification of their powers will occupy two or three days. On Monday, however, the Convention, it is thought, will begin to act—perhaps before.

Thus is the second Legislature terminated, after having occasioned a second Revolution, not less fatal to the Constitution decreed by the first, than that Constitution had been to the Government which had ruled France for fourteen centuries.—Thus, after more than three years of troubles, agitations, murders, and crimes in short of every description, does France still plunge deeper and deeper into the horrors of anarchy—placed betwixt powerful enemies, whose armies already cover several of her provinces, and Legislators devoid of morality or principle, who have established themselves upon thousands of victims sacrificed to the vengeance, or rather to the imaginary terrors of a governing faction.

The triumph of PETION in no degree affects the situation of the virtuous Citizens. There was but a solitary choice betwixt him and ROBERTSPIERRE [*sic*]. They are both the chiefs and secret movers of the scenes of carnage and destruction the present month has witnessed. They were guided, each in his own way, by different motives; but the massacres were not on that account the less to be imputed to them. PETION has now the advantage of his opponent—but will he preserve it? This is a problem which can only be resolved by events; for every calculation which has for its basis the popular opinion alone, disconcerts conjecture, and can simply afford a result when the facts have taken place.

Besides, the 20th, for which day new massacres had been announced, has passed over in perfect tranquillity, by means of the measures which were taken to prevent every accident. The incendiary *placards* of *Marat* were productive of no bad effect; and the MINISTERS, particularly the one who presides over the Interior Department, whom this frantic writer pointed out as sacrifices to the fury of the people, are as tranquil as the Sieur DANTON, upon whom he lavishes his favours.

PETION, before he quitted his Mayoralty, denounced *Marat* to the Commons, as one of the principal authors of the last assassinations. It will be a matter of some curiosity to see what steps the National Convention will take, to revenge on this occasion the national honour,—whether a similar sensation will penetrate to the hearts of these great Legislators, or whether they will not regard it as beneath the sublimity of their functions to descend to these minute details.

September 26th, 1792

FRENCH REFUGEE CLERGY

We understand the Subscribers for the relief of the distressed French Clergy, Refugees in the British dominions, are proceeding in that humane undertaking. The extent, however, of the relief to be afforded to these distressed people and the manner in which it should be dispensed, must require a deliberate consideration. These unfortunate men fly to our shores for refuge from an indiscriminate persecution and from death; they therefore have a claim on our humanity, for such assistance as may save them from perishing, distinct from all considerations of politics or their religion; but then this assistance should be afforded in such a manner as not to be prejudicial to the working part of our fellow subjects, who as our countrymen and brethren have the first claim on our bounty.

It has been apprehended by some, that the great influx of French into this kingdom, or at least into the metropolis may have the effect of increasing the general price of provisions, a circumstance which when their numbers are considered is impossible; but though the French Clergy form but a small portion of the whole number of Emigrants here, the subscribers to their particular relief appear to think that it will be better to remove the greater part of them from the capital.—To this end we learn, that they have applied to, and obtained from Government an offer of his Majesty's House at Winchester; and a survey is now taking of the building, as to the state of its repair, and its capacity to receive a number of these unfortunate men.

The number of French Clergy now in London, is estimated at about 900, of whom a considerable number are preparing to go to Ostend, and other places out of these dominions, and of the remainder not more than one third are in such distress as to want the necessaries of life; if we calculate that 500 are dispersed in the different towns and villages in England, and that no more than the same proportion of these are in absolute distress. The number is by no means such as to alarm us on our own account; and when we consider that learned men and particularly the Clergy are above all others the least able when in want to procure a maintenance for themselves; when we recollect also, that to solicit and distribute alms has till now been considered as an essential part of their duty as Clergymen; we cannot surely for a moment hesitate in relieving objects like these, reduced by unavoidable necessity, not by any crime of their own, to solicit at our hands, in a foreign land, for the means of preserving life, mere food and shelter.

On September 20th, the French volunteer army under Dumouriez faced the advancing Prussians at Valmy, near Sainte-Ménehould, and beat them off. The Duke of Brunswick began his long retreat to the frontier. The Times, *now and in succeeding weeks, refused to believe in the French victory.*

October 5th, 1792

We have little or no information to offer to the public in confirmation or contradiction of the important news concerning the fate of M. DUMOURIER's army, the report remains precisely as it did on Monday last; if we except, that neither the French

October 5th, 1792

Gazettes of Monday, nor private letters written on Sunday in Paris, make any mention of the affair. Every circumstance which relates to either the French or the Combined Armies is so wrapt up in mystery, and there is so little information to be depended on from either, that the public opinion is lost in conjecture. Indeed there has been no authentic news from the Generals of the Northern armies communicated to the National Assembly since the 23rd inst. On Sunday last, M. *Servan* asserted in the National Assembly, that he had received no intelligence whatever from the combined armies, nor from the South.

In the course of yesterday, we had opportunities of seeing several persons who must have learnt any material intelligence, had it been received; but they know as little of the matter as we do.—The private letters from Paris mention only those circumstances respecting the armies, which are publicly known through the National Assembly.

We continue in the same opinion as was expressed in our paper of yesterday, viz. that the critical situation of *Dumourier's* army, and the knowledge of its retreat having been cut off by the forced marches of the combined armies, has given room for well founded conjecture, that Dumourier has been surrounded,—and hence appears to originate the report; that such news may be confirmed appears highly probable.

The French Gazettes still teem with absurd reports, that the KING of PRUSSIA and Duke of BRUNSWICK have offered terms of accommodation to the French GENERAL from necessity, and that the heads of both parties were in the most social intercourse, and had dined together. The public are to form their own judgment of these matters, but to us they appear too inconsistent even to comment on their probability.

The Flanders Mail due this day will, we hope, unveil this mystery.

The Convention met on September 21st, and abolished the Monarchy by unanimous decree. The formal duty of the Convention was to frame a constitution, but its sessions widened the gulf between the Girondins and the radical Jacobins, including Marat, Danton and Robespierre, whose higher seats in the hall earned them the name of the 'Montagne'. The Times, using French newspapers, kept its readers informed of the debates.

October 1st, 1792

. . . "Yes, Gentlemen," exclaimed M. *La Source*, "I have observed the uneasiness of several citizens on a report which has been spread, that two thirds of the Convention wish to establish a Dictatorship; and I appeal to M. *Merlin*, whether it be not true, that he himself told me, in a Committee of *Surveillance*, that I should be assassinated at my post, and that a party exists which is determined to rid itself of all the Members who have not displayed any energy. Yes, it exists—I denounce to the Tribunal a party which aspires to the dictatorial power, and which aims at establishing a despotism over France, after having awed the National Convention. I dread those who give arbitrary orders; who, whilst assassinations were committed in the prisons, issued mandates of arrest against the citizens, against eight of my colleagues in the Legislative Assembly. I dread this scum of the human race, vomited by France, and let loose against us *by some Brunswick*. The citizens of Paris are unquestionably the safeguard of the National Convention; but I think that Paris should at the same time have the eighty-third part of the influence only in this respect. I speak it with courage; I have already removed the veil, and should I be able to discover the plots which are on foot, I will repair to this Tribunal to denouce them to all France: for I have no manner of doubt but the same power which has annihilated the despotism of LOUIS the Sixteenth, will soon thunder out its Dictatorships and Triumvirates. Neither poignards nor proscriptions can prevent me from unmasking publicly the turpitude of this party!"—(Loud applauses.)

"ROBERSPIERRE," exclaimed a Member, "is the chief of this faction which aspires to the Dictatorship. He is the traitor, and has entrusted his project to M. *Barbaroux*."—(A violent tumult.)

M. *Danton*, in a long harrangue, demanded that the accuser should sign his accusation. "Should it be attended," cried he, "by the forfeiture of the head of my dearest friend, still my country must be avenged. I know that there exists in the Republic a man who is the *Royau*[1] of the Revolution—this man is *Marat*. Too long have I been charged with being the author of his placards and writings. But on this occasion I call on our President. I must,

[1] The 'Royau' mentioned by Danton was Royon, a right-wing journalist who had been arrested in April.

81

however, do justice to *Marat*; it appears to me that the splenetic turn of his character, that his subterraneous life, has inspired him to write these libels which render him *such a pest to society.*"

M. *Danton* now justified his personal conduct, and the deputation of Paris, against the accusations of the preceding speakers. He demanded *the penalty of death against any one who should speak of a dictatorship, and proposed by a decree to declare France indivisible, as well as the unity of the national representation, and that of the Executive Power.* The Convention rose up in the midst of the loudest applause.

M. *Roberspierre* now mounted the tribune, and spoke at considerable length, but in a strain of egotism that disgusted those who heard him. Instead of replying to the accusations thrown out against him, or denying them, he entered into a history of his public life, and the services he had rendered his country, by exposing the plots that had been meditated to overthrow the Constitution. He did not, however, think proper to name who were the authors of the conspiracies he alluded to. At length the assembly tired of hearing him, as he continued to evade the answer to the charges made against him, began to be noisy. . . .

M. *d'Osselin* cried out, "prevent us from declaring all you have done by telling us what you wish to do. Declare to us whether you have not advised a dictatorship." M. *Roberspierre* interrupted this challenge offered to him, by continuing to expatiate on his public life.

M. *Barbaroux* confirmed the accusation made against *Roberspierre*. "We were called," said he, "to *Roberspierre's* house. M. *Panis* described him to us as a virtuous citizen, who deserved to be called to the dictatorship of France. I have since discovered the horrid plot of creating a dictatorship in the disorganizing conduct of the Commons of Paris, which sends its Commissioners to every part of France to bring about a want of subordination, and which issues its mandates of arrest against the Minister *Roland.*"

Eight hundred Marseillois, chosen from among the most ardent of the patriots, appeared at the bar of the Convention, stating that their purpose was to defend Paris and their rulers; six hundred livres were given to each. They were accompanied by two hundred horsemen equipped at their own expence, and made the following address to the Convention: "We, deputed by the City of Marseilles, shall pray incessantly for the union of all parts of France, and for the annihilation of *robbers* and *dictators*, of whatever party they may be. We will oblige the Commons of Paris to return to its functions; but will prevent at the same time the metropolis from being blockaded by the enemy. We will point out a City where those we have left behind us will continue our labours, but, for our own parts, we will die here. Let the Federative Convention be banished; if *Roberspierre* has served the Country by his writings, we have served it with our blood. We shall see whether those who have dared to paste up placards know how to die."

Several deputies spoke in favour of the denunciation. M. *Cambon* declared that he had seen posted up in Paris a paper, signed *Marat*, in which it was said that there was no other mode of saving the country, unless by a Triumvirate. He traced the proscriptions exercised against the deputies, and the public service of the treasury impeded by the seals which the Commons had placed upon it, in violation of the laws.

M. *Panis* endeavoured to justify himself upon the charge made against him, and felt a conviction that the conspiracy formed at the *Thuilleries* was calculated to overthrow the liberty of the Republic. He had concerted measures with the Marseillois, with M. *Barbaroux* himself, and had delivered cartouches to the former without the consent of the Mayor. He further protested that he had never wished either for a Dictatorship or a Triumvirate.

M. *Marat.*—"I have a great number of enemies in the Convention."

Several Members.—"Yes, we are all, we are all your enemies."

M. *Marat.*—"I declare that the citizens *Danton* and *Roberspierre* have constantly scouted the idea of a Dictatorship. If any one is culpable for having thought that, to disconcert the plots of a corrupt Court, it was necessary to place the avenging sword of the people in the hands of a Dictator, it is I, I myself; and if it is a crime, I call down on my own head the vengeance of the nation."

M. *Vergniaud* denounced the address of the Commons to the Eighty-three Departments, and demanded the punishment of those who had signed it, provided they should acknowledge their signatures.

M. *Boileau* presented a new Placard of M. *Marat*'s production, importing, that if the National Convention should not form a Constitution within a fortnight, there would be an end of Liberty; and that the only safe expedient would be to appoint a Dictator.

Marat acknowledged the Placard, but excused himself by stating that he had written it ten days ago. At this time he paid the necessary homage to the Convention, in proof of which he produced a new Journal conformable to its principles.

The order of the day was called for, and adopted. M. *Marat* now presented himself to the Tribunal, with a pistol in his hand held towards his temple: "Had you passed," said he, "a Decree of accusation against me, I should have blown out my brains. This, then, is the reward of my labours, of all I have done for my country."

(Such was the farcical conclusion of this scene, which seemed to threaten a tragical *denouement.*—We know, however, that for a long time the quarrels of the patriots have terminated in this way.)

On December 3rd, the Convention resolved on the trial of the King. The Times *devoted many pages to the proceedings.*

The trial ended in open votes, with stated opinions from each deputy. Out of 720 votes, 683 found Louis Capet guilty of conspiracy against the Revolution. The final vote, on the penalty, went on all night until six in the morning.

Thomas Paine, author of The Rights of Man, *was one of six radical Englishmen and Scotsmen granted honorary citizenship in 1792. He was the only one to become a member of the Convention.*

January 23rd, 1793

.   .   .

Roberspierre—"Because you have established yourselves the judges of Louis, without the usual forms, are you less his judges? You cannot separate your quality of Judge from that of Legislator. These two qualities are indivisible. You have acknowledged the crimes of the tyrant. It is your duty to punish them. No consideration should make you hesitate respecting the punishment reserved for the greatest criminal that ever existed. I vote for the punishment of death."

84

Danton—"I am a Republican, and do not hesitate respecting the choice of that punishment reserved for Louis the last. You ought to strike a terror into tyrants—I vote for the punishment of death."

Manuel—"I vote for the imprisonment of the tyrant during the continuance of the war, in that place where the victims of his despotism languished; and for his expulsion when peace shall be secured."

Robert—"I vote for death; and if any regret remains, it is, that my competence does not extend to all tyrants. I would condemn them all to death."

Freron—"Were it possible that the majority should determine upon him imprisonment, I would move that a veil might be thrown over the bust of Brutus. I vote for death."

Osselin—"I regret that the laws of my country pronounce the punishment of death against those who are guilty of great crimes. The tedious punishment of imprisonment for life would be much more beneficial to society. But as the law has not yet been changed, I vote that Louis may be put to death."

Barrere—"The tree of liberty does not flourish, unless moistened with the blood of Kings. I vote for death."

. . .

Anarcharsis Cloots—"In the name of the Human Race I vote for the death of Louis."

Thomas Paine—"I vote for the provisional confinement of Louis, and for his expulsion after the war."

Brissot—"It would have been desirable that the punishment to be inflicted on Louis should have been pronounced by the whole nation. It would have been the best method of carrying along with us the sentiments of the neighbouring nations, and of defeating the projects of the tyrants of Europe, who desire the punishment of Louis, in order more successfully to excite indignation and hatred against the National Convention. But as the Assembly have thought proper to reject the Appeal to the People, I am now of opinion, that the only way of avoiding the dangers which threaten us, is to pronounce the punishment of death against Louis, and defer its execution to the moment when the people shall have sanctioned the Constitution which we shall present them. I know that, in some sense, the opinion which I deliver may be calumniated; I have only to offer, in reply to my enemies, my honourable poverty. The moment, perhaps, is not distant, when I shall bequeath it to my children; but while I live I will exert myself, with all my power, for the maintenance of order; without which a Republic can only be a combination of ruffians. I declare as a man who has a profound knowledge of our success, of our resources, and of those of the powers who threaten us, that we have nothing to fear from Kings and their satellites; and, I add, that if we do not destroy that system of disorganization which has raised its audacious head, the Republic is lost."

.   .   .

Tranquillity was restored in the Assembly. The tumult had been so great a few minutes before, as to force the President to put on his hat. The Deputy who had been indisposed, voted for detention and banishment.

"The Assembly is composed of seven hundred and forty-five Members—one of these is dead, six indisposed, two absent without cause, and censured in the Minutes, conformable to the decree, eleven absent upon commissions, and four who do not vote, making, in all, twenty-three Members who have given no opinion. The number of votes is thus reduced to seven hundred and twenty-one. In order that there may be a majority, it is necessary that there should be an union of three hundred and sixty one suffrages. Twenty one Members have voted for death, with the demand of a discussion on the period of his execution; one has voted for death, with the reserve of its commutation or delay; two for death, not to be carried into execution till peace, unless in the case of invasion of the French territory, in which instance, to be inflicted within twenty-four hours after such invasion has taken place; two for chains; three hundred and nineteen for imprisonment and banishment; three hundred and sixty-six for death!"

The *President* then, lowering the tone of his voice, amidst the most profound and awful silence, proceeded to pronounce the following Sentence:

"I DECLARE, THEN, IN THE NAME OF THE CONVENTION, THAT THE PUNISHMENT WHICH IT PRONOUNCES AGAINST LOUIS CAPET IS—DEATH!"

The three Defenders of Louis Capet were then admitted to the Bar. One of them, *de Seze*, said,

"Citizens, Representatives, the law and your decrees have entrusted to us the sacred function of the defence of Louis. We come, with regret, to present to you the last act of our function. Louis has given to us his express charge to read to you a letter signed with his own hand, of which the following is a copy:

LETTER FROM LOUIS.

I owe to my honour, I owe to my family, not to subscribe to a sentence which declares me guilty of a crime, with which I cannot accuse myself. In consequence, I appeal to the Nation, from the sentence of its Representatives; and I commit, by these presents, to the fidelity of my Defenders, to make known to the National Convention this appeal, by all the means in their power, and to demand, that mention of it be made in the minutes of their sittings.

Given at Paris, the 16th of January, 1793.

(Signed) 'LOUIS.'

De Seze then resumed the discourse. He reminded the Assembly, that the Decreee of Death had only been pronounced by a majority of five voices, while the other part of the Assembly were of opinion, that the safety of the country required another decision. He warmly conjured them to examine a-new the question of Appeal, and to grant to humanity, and the interest of the State, all that justice might not seem imperiously to claim.

The King was executed on January 21st.

January 25th, 1793

EXECUTION OF LOUIS XVI. KING OF THE FRENCH

By an express which arrived yesterday morning from Messrs. *Fector* and Co. at Dover, we learn the following particulars of the King's execution:

At six o'clock on Monday morning, the KING went to take a farewell of the QUEEN and ROYAL FAMILY. After staying with them some time, and taking a very affectionate farewell of them, the KING descended from the tower of the Temple, and entered the Mayor's carriage, with his confessor and two Members of the Municipality, and passed slowly along the Boulevards which led from the Temple to the place of execution. All women were prohibited from appearing in the streets, and all persons from being seen at their windows. A strong guard cleared the procession.

The greatest tranquillity prevailed in every street through which the procession passed. About half past nine, the King arrived at the place of execution, which was in the *Place de Louis XV*, between the pedestal which formerly supported the statue of his grandfather, and the promenade of the Elysian Fields. LOUIS mounted the scaffold with composure, and that modest intrepidity peculiar to oppressed innocence, the trumpets sounding and drums beating during the whole time. He made a sign of wishing to harangue the multitude, when the drums ceased, and Louis spoke these few words. *I die innocent; I pardon my enemies; I only sanctioned upon compulsion the Civil Constitution of the Clergy.*—He was proceeding, but the beating of the drums drowned his voice. His executioners then laid hold of him, and an instant after, his head was separated from his body; this was about a quarter past ten o'clock.

After the execution, the people threw their hats up in the air, and cried out *Vive la Nation!* Some of them endeavoured to seize the body, but it was removed by a strong guard to the Temple, and the lifeless remains of the King were exempted from those outrages which his Majesty had experienced during his life.

The King was attended on the scaffold by an Irish Priest as his Confessor, not choosing to be accompanied by one who had taken the National oath. He was dressed in a brown great coat, white waistcoat and black breeches, and his hair was powdered.

When M. de *Malsherbes* announced to LOUIS, the fatal sentence of Death. "Ah!" exclaimed the Monarch, "I shall then at length be delivered from this cruel suspense."

The decree imported that LOUIS should be beheaded in the *Place de Carouzel,* but reasons of public safety induced the Executive Council to prefer the *Place de la Revolution,* formerly the *Place de Louis* XV.

.   .   .

Unquestionably, the blood of this unfortunate Monarch will invoke vengeance on his murderers. This is not the cause of Monarchs only, it is the cause of every nation on the face of the earth. All potentates owe it to their individual honour, but still more strongly to the happiness of their people collectively, to crush these savage Regicides in their dens, who aim at the ruin of all nations, and the destruction of all Governments. It is not by feeble efforts only, that we can hope to exterminate these inhuman wretches. Experience has proved them to be ineffectual. Armed with fire and sword, we must penetrate into the recesses of this land of blood and carnage. Louis might still have been living, had neighbouring Princes acted with that energy and expedition, which the case required.

January 26th, 1793

We continue to have reason to suppose, that on Monday next, the WAR with FRANCE will be taken into consideration in the House of Commons. We believe it was yesterday finally determined on in the Cabinet Council, which sat at Buckingham House from twelve till two, and again at Lord GRENVILLE's Office from three to six o'clock.

Notwithstanding Government has taken every measure which humanity could suggest to procure volunteer seamen, and has been tolerably successful, we fear that the urgency of the armament will make it absolutely necessary to issue PRESS WARRANTS.

We learn that an embargo has been laid on in several of the French ports, and probably there may be the same necessity for doing so in our own.

The departure of M. de CHAUVELIN,[1] which we announced on Thursday as likely to take place within 48 hours, is now confirmed; and e're this paper is read by the public, this Jacobin emissary will be on his return to France. Our Government only waited for the news of the murder of his late most CHRISTIAN MAJESTY to give M. de Chauvelin notice to quit the kingdom, which was done by a letter sent by Lord GRENVILLE to him on Thursday evening, in consequence of an order of Council of the same day.—Chauvelin had the insolence to say, he would return an answer to this letter.

The answer given by Lord GRENVILLE to the last letter of CHAUVELIN, expressed, "that the explanations attempted to be made on the *Alien Bill* and the opening of the *Scheldt*, instead of being satisfactory, were considered as fresh insult and aggression, and that it was needless for him to send any more such letters."

---

[1] Chauvelin was the French Ambassador.

The 'opening' of the Scheldt was not only a violation of Dutch rights over the estuary but a direct threat to British trade and military security. When French warships forced the river, it meant that Antwerp, the proverbial 'pistol pointed at the heart of England', could now be used as an anti-British naval or even invasion base. No single act did more to drive the reluctant Pitt away from his policy of neutrality. In December 1792, a month after the opening of the Scheldt, he introduced the Alien Bill, empowering the Secretary of State to restrict the activities of resident or visiting foreigners and if necessary to expel them. The Alien Bill, designed to control French 'revolutionists' and their agents, was the direct ancestor of modern British practice towards immigrants and politically inconvenient foreigners. It was in the debate on the Bill that Burke whanged a dagger down on the floor of the House, claiming that it was one of thousands being forged in Birmingham by revolutionists.

January 28th, 1793

FURTHER PARTICULARS OF
THE EXECUTION OF LOUIS XVI

EXTRACT OF A PRIVATE LETTER FROM PARIS, BY A GENTLEMAN WHO WAS A SPECTATOR OF THE EXECUTION OF LOUIS XVI.

"I have been a spectator of one of the most tragical sights that ever my eyes witnessed; but the circumstance was of too much importance to allow me to be absent from the spectacle. Upwards of 60,000 horse and foot were on duty.

"The Mayor's carriage being arrived at the place of execution, drew up close to the scaffold. The two executioners approached the coach. The King and his Confessor then got out of it. The King, on mounting the scaffold, instantly took off his stock himself, as well as his great coat, and unfastened his shirt collar. His hair had been clubbed up close like an Abbe's, in order that no indignity might be offered him, or that it should occasion delay by hanging loose. The executioner went to tie up his arms which the King recoiled at, but it was soon done.—The executioner then took up a large pair of scissors to cut off his hair. The King appeared mortified at what was doing, and said, 'I have put all right'—The executioner, however, cut the hair off.

"His Majesty then said, 'I pardon my enemies—May my death be useful to the nation.' The executioners then placed him to be beheaded; the King recoiled, and said—'Another moment, that I may speak to the people.' The *Aid de Camp* to the Commandant, *Santerre*, then said to *Henri Sausson*, the executioner, 'Do your duty.' The wedge then slipt, and his head was instantly off. Two minutes after the head was shewn to the people, and, with the body, thrown into a long basket, and taken to the Church-yard of St. Magdelaine, where it was immediately buried.

"The time of the arrival of the carriage at the scaffold, to the King's mounting, was precisely ten minutes, and six minutes after he was executed; for very particular orders had been given, that as little time as possible should be employed in the execution. In nine minutes after, the body was removed.

"From a particular acquaintance with some of the Municipal Officers, I learn, that, on the Thursday preceding the execution, the King was permitted to see the Queen, for the first time for a month. It was in the presence of six Municipal officers. LOUIS said to the Queen—'I am told the Convention has condemned me to death.—I exhort you to prepare yourself for the like fate. I pray you to bear up the minds of our children to meet the like sacrifice, for we shall all be victims.'

"A dead silence reigns in the public streets of Paris; but all the playhouses are open, and the city is illuminated every night, as if the French wished to make their wickedness more visible."

February 1st, 1793

MASSACRE OF THE KING OF FRANCE
This Day is published, price 6d.

An account of the Tragic Event, with an Engraving of La Guillotine, or the Beheading Machine, by which he suffered, January 21, 1793. This Plate accurately describes the fatal instrument with which he was sacrificed.

Printed at the Minerva Press for Wm. Lane, Leadenhall Street; and sold by E. Harlow, Pall-Mall; Edwards, Bond-Street; Shepherd and Reynolds, Oxford-Street; Wesley, Strand; Symonds, Paternoster-row; Richardson, Royal Exchange; and all other Booksellers in England, Scotland, Ireland, &c.

* * Such as will take 100 may have them for 2 guineas. Where may be had also, an exact and authenticated Copy of his last Will and Testament, price 2d.

ACTS
OF THE FRENCH EXISTING GOVERNMENT
TOWARDS THE ENGLISH NATION

A brief abstract of the proceedings of the French towards the English Government, since the scandalous detention of Louis XVI, will no doubt be extremely acceptable to our readers at the present moment.

The ENGLISH AMBASSADOR was subjected in the month of August to forms, to refusals, and to an inquisition, inconsistent with the character of a Representative of the KING of GREAT BRITAIN.

The English, at that time in France, had not the liberty of quitting when they chose, a country, where the lives of individuals was abandoned to arbitrary fury, and to assassins who make a joke of the crime of murder.

Some were seized in the night, and dragged to prison, at a time when the massacres of September were already resolved on. They in vain claimed their priviledge of being subjects of Great Britain, and those who escaped only owed their safety to chance; and even of these, two were afterwards massacred.

Whole Societies of British subjects (the Irish Priests) were compelled to fly from death, and abandon their houses, which they had purchased under the protection of the King of Great Britain, and the faith of treaties. Under that liberty of conscience, proclaimed by France herself, they peaceably pursued their studies, and religiously exercised their worship.

English travellers were arrested, insulted, and menaced; English women were placed under a guard of fusileers; others were plundered, and one lady experienced ignominious insults, worse than death.

Persons possessed of property, who by treaty, and even by the French Constitution, might purchase, acquire, and contract in France, were classed as emigrants, because they returned to their own country and their families; their property was seized, their revenues confiscated, and their goods sold.

These individual injuries have been crowned by acts of universal injustice, which have violated whatever, since the existence of society, has been held sacred; and which have trampled on every thing, which morality and universal reason exacts, according to the law of nations.

The French have plotted, they have conspired, nay at this very moment they conceived the project of overturning our superb Constitution, which for a century past has elevated Great Britain to hold the first rank in the scale of great and opulent nations.

They have sent over a malignant band of levellers, hired to draw down upon the English all those scourges which have desolated their own country. Different parties have been distributed in England, Scotland, and Ireland, and even in the British colonies. A sacriligious hierarchy has been established amongst these apostles of crime and discord. Every society has had its Chief, with many others under him, and each have been in proportion liberally rewarded, and furnished with the means to corrupt other wicked and ambitious men, such as will be found under even the wisest and best regulated governments. All the Chiefs have corresponded with each other; emissaries have incessantly gone from one place to another, disseminating incendiary libels and perfidious exhortations. These have returned to France, and reported their progress; and have from thence returned to England with fresh instructions and fresh funds.

All these facts are substantially authenticated; the chiefs, the agents, the corresponding societies, the times of meeting, the journies, the resolutions, nay even the very day when all these plots were to have been executed is well ascertained.

It is perfectly well known, which of these agents had unlimited credit; which of them received so much per week, per month, per day. It is clearly ascertained, that the project was formed of storming the Tower, of pillaging the arsenal, of attacking the houses of persons of property, and the public offices; in a word, to level at one blow every branch of the British Constitution. Either Saturday, the 1st, or Wednesday, the 5th of December, was the day fixed on for this horrid project. The pattern of the daggers, with which these seditious villains were to be armed, was found at the house of a Frenchman, and 20,000 were so far manufactured, that they could have been completed within 36 hours.

A Member of the NATIONAL CONVENTION is known, who thinking there was too much delay in the execution of these plans, wrote to one of his agents in London, that *it was not thus*

93

that he ought to labour, and that he did not earn the money of the Republic.

Other Members of the Convention are also known, who had endeavoured to arm and excite the negroes in the English colonies to *destroy our power in the West Indies at any rate.*

An emissary, who remained in London only 24 hours, and then set off on his mission to the Hague, in order to create an insurrection in Holland, is also well known.

Another emissary is also known, who wrote from France about the middle of last November, asserting *that an insurrection was upon the point of bursting forth in London,* and who again wrote towards the middle of December, *that there were no further hopes at that instance of effecting this project.*

The *Chief* is also known, who informed his agents in London, *that the first attempt having failed, they must be very cautious in what manner they conducted a second.*

The *name and number of the French artillery-men,* who had received orders to embark for Ireland on Monday the 17th of December last; the name of the leader who countermanded and sent them back to France, whither he himself also returned: all these facts are clearly ascertained.

So sure were the French of success, that at Paris they threw off the mask. In the Convention, on the 28th of November, many individuals, calling themselves British subjects, appeared at the bar, to blaspheme the British Constitution, and to announce, that *perhaps in a very short time, it would exist no longer.* They boasted of being rebels to their King and their country, and the Convention loaded them with applause, nay the President, in his answer, even presumed to invite all the subjects of Great Britain to revolt against the laws of their Country, their King, and the Parliament; and he had the audacity to declare, *that Royalty was expiring, and that a devouring flame was upon the point of consuming the throne of Great Britain.* Fresh applause was bestowed, and it was decreed, that the printing of this declaration would give a solemn character, and extensive publicity to this double act of treason and hostility.

Whilst the French Government was thus secretly plotting the ruin of England, the French Ambassador, *in the name of the French people, gave the King of Great Britain a formal assurance that every thing relative to the rights of his Britannic Majesty would be regarded with the most particular and scrupulous attention; he promised that the most exemplary severity should be exer-*

94

cized against those, who dared for a moment to foment or favour insurrection against the established order of the country, by interfering, in any manner, in the interior politics of neighbouring states, under the pretext of proselytism, which, being recommended to countries at peace with France, would be an obvious violation of the rights of nations!!!

On November 19th,1792, the Convention had offered fraternal assistance to all peoples seeking their freedom, and on December 15th passed detailed measures for installing popular democracy in all 'liberated' countries.

In March, the advance by Dumouriez into Holland was outflanked. The French were beaten back into Belgium. Dumouriez, now disillusioned with the Revolution, tried to revoke the reforms in Belgium which had been imposed by France, quarrelled with Danton and defected to the enemy. In Paris, the news of his retreat touched off a fresh storm of patriotic emotion; in the 'March Days', women, civil servants and artisans left for the front. Counterrevolution broke out in the Vendée region of the west, and at Lyon.

March 15th, 1793

PARIS, MONDAY MARCH 11

[EXTRACT OF A PRIVATE LETTER]

"The convulsion I anticipated to you in my last, has already broken out, but not with those terrible consequences which must soon follow: the destruction of the press has been the first object of the fury of the Orleans party, preparatory to the public acknowledgment of their Hero as DICTATOR. The printing office of *Gorsas* has been the first to suffer, as he was the most violent enemy of all others to *Marat* and his crew. The printing office of *Condorcet* has likewise been destroyed. The rage of the party of the *Mountain* against the Republicans is excessive, and I have no doubt but they will be sacrificed in their turn.

"In consequence of the unfortunate news from our armies, the Convention has invited all the citizens capable of bearing arms, to fly to the frontiers to the relief of their brethren in Belgia. All the places of public amusement have been ordered to be shut; the drum has beat for each citizen to repair to his Section, and by order of the Mayor, the *black flag,* which denotes that the country is in danger, is flying on the steeple of the church of *Notre Dame.*

"The following Proclamation was yesterday published with great solemnity through all the streets and cross streets of Paris.

TO ARMS, CITIZENS, TO ARMS!

If you hesitate, ALL IS LOST!!!

'A considerable portion of the Republic is invaded; *Aix-la-Chapelle, Liege, Brussels,* may be, even now, in the possession of the enemy; the heavy artillery, the baggage, the treasure of the army have been obliged to fall back precipitately toward *Valenciennes,* the only town which can for a moment impede the progress of the enemy. All that cannot follow will be thrown into the *Meuse.* General *Dumourier* is making conquests in Holland; but if considerable levies of recruits do not support him, DUMOURIER, *and with him the flower of the French armies, may be irretrievably lost.*

'PARISIANS! Consider the magnitude of the danger. Will you permit the enemy again to ravage this land of liberty, to desolate with fire your towns and your villas?

'PARISIANS! It is particularly against you, that this abominable war is directed. It is your wives, your children, whom they wish to massacre. It is Paris that they mean to reduce to ashes. Remember that the insolent BRUNSWICK has sworn not to leave one stone upon another.

'PARISIANS! Once more save the Commonwealth; once more set an example; *rise—arm—march;* and these bands of slaves will again recoil before you. The last effort is required; it must be a terrible—a finishing blow. This campaign decides the fate of the world. Kings must be terrified; they must be exterminated. *Men of the 14th of July, and the 5th of October; Men of the 10th of August, rouze!!!*

'Your brethren, your children, pursued by the enemy, perhaps surrounded by them, invoke your assistance; your brethren, your children, massacred in the plains of *Champaigne,* and under the smoking ruins of *Lille,* your brothers killed at *Jemappe—Rise and revenge their death.*

'Let all our arms in the Sections be occupied. Citizens! repair thither, and swear to save the country—save it. Woe to him that hesitates. Let thousands of men march from Paris. This is the moment of deadly combat between men and Kings—between slavery and liberty.

(Signed) 'PACHE'.'

"This Proclamation, as you may judge, is well calculated to rouse the spirit of the people, but their zeal is a good deal slackened by the recollection of the pillage which took place the other day. They tremble, lest in leaving their shops and trades, their families should be exposed to the depredations of the Agrarian law-givers. There is likewise a general inquietude about the prisons, which are menaced with a renewal of the scenes of the 2d and 3d of September. There is a secret Committee held, where these projects are prepared.

"The Jacobins have demanded, that all the Ministers should be dismissed, and that others should immediately be chosen from among their own faction. The whole power of the country, is evidently passing into the hands of this desperate and sanguinary faction.

"The news from Lyons is not more favourable. The deputation from the Convention is reported to have been received by a discharge of artillery from the ramparts."

The Convention being in theory a constituent assembly, France had no formal government. Power belonged to those who could prevail in the Convention and especially in its committees. It was evident that the struggle between 'Girondins' and the Robespierre faction would only be settled by another Parisian rising. The 'Gironde' majority in the Convention was not effective, and Marat's impeachment, mentioned here, ended in acquittal. The rumour that Danton was playing a double game, picked up by The Times, *remains unproved to this day.*

May 2nd, 1793

The news we have received from PARIS, and indeed the opinion of well informed persons in this country has almost universally tended to this belief, that the party of the *Gironde,* which consists of *Le Brun, Brissot,* and those who at present have the charge of the Executive Power in France, would finally be crushed by the more tremendous and bloody faction of the *Jacobins,* entitled the *Mountain,* who have most of the Sections in Paris and the mobs in the provinces at their command.

The affairs of FRANCE have so often baffled every speculation of the politician and the philosopher, and the convulsions in that country have varied both in form and substance so often, that the mind is unsettled on what principle to fix for the probable termination of so many disorders. We therefore are extremely cautious in giving any opinion on the subject, especially one which is so novel and unexpected; we have however very good authority for what we are about to state:

The party of *Gironde* can carry 450 votes in the National Convention, and is said to become stronger every day. The minority is formidable, only in having all the cut-throats and rabble at its obedience, and it is much weakened at the present moment by having a number of its adherents absent on different deputations to the armies, &c. the Commissioners of which are almost all *Jacobins.* It is this circumstance that made the majority in the Convention so large in the vote against MARAT, and caused the decree of banishment against that illustrious villain *Egalité*.

We are now told that *Le Brun,* and some others of his party, have had sufficient address to weaken the *Mountain* faction by bribing over to their interest, some of its leading Members, of whom we may reckon *Danton* and *Lacroix* as principals. As it was necessary however to conduct this business with great secrecy, it was agreed that Danton should still continue to thunder out his anathemas against the *Girondists,* in order to blind the Tribunes; but according to our information, this fellow has been bought over, and will shew himself in his true colours, whenever the proper and not very distant moment shall arrive to exterminate *Marat's* gang effectually.

In this state of affairs, we are very confidently informed that *Le Brun,* who is lately made PERMANENT President of the Executive Council and is certainly the cleverest man among them, has proposed as the first necessary step to settle a permanent government in France, that an attempt should be made to detach Great Britain from the general combination of powers, and that

98

he has actually sent over two persons to this country to convey his letters to Lord GRENVILLE, as the preliminary step to a negotiation, which are said to *have been actually received*. If this is the fact, we may suppose that they contain a *carte blanche*, and that it is left to our Cabinet almost to dictate the terms of a separate peace; or to interest itself as a mediator.

At the end of May, the explosion was close. Hébert was among seven men arrested for planning insurrection, but released when the 'Girondins' were defeated in the Convention. The President (Speaker) was the Girondin Isnard; by 'covering' his head with a hat, he intended to suspend the session.

June 13th, 1793

PARIS, MAY 30

(EXTRACT OF A LETTER.)

"The storm seems to gather in the bosom of the Convention. Such tumultuous scenes were never before witnessed. It is much apprehended that the sparks from this assemblage of combustible materials will fly to the distant parts of the kingdom, and kindle a civil war. It is in this Assembly that we hear public challenges given, and the most opprobrious epithets used by one Member against the other; all is noise and confusion; and thus is the Sanctuary of the Laws and of Liberty turned into an Amphitheatre of Gladiators.

"You will see by the papers I send you, what has passed in the Convention. I was present at the sitting of the 27th instant, and was witness to all the scandalous tumults which passed on that day. The President was covered several times, without being heard, or even attended to. His voice was drowned in the cries and hisses from the tribunes; and, he observed, that not being able to re-establish good order, he was about to write to all the Departments to acquaint the People of the little respect and decency that was shewn to their Representatives. When he finished his letter, a Member from the *Mountain* snatched it from his hand, tore it to pieces, and rubbed his hand over the President's face, as a mark of contempt; at the same time dragging him from his chair.

99

"You may conceive what tumult this occasioned. For several minutes nothing was to be heard but groanings and hisses. At length the President was escorted back to his seat, and an armed force was called into the Hall of the Convention. The noise continued until the principal actors had tired their lungs. . . .

"The arrest of the Citizen *Hebert*, a Member of the Commons, has been the occasion of more riot and confusion than any circumstance which has happened for some time past. The cause of his arrest was—for having published a periodical paper, entitled *Le Pere du Chene*; in which, following the example of *Marat*, he preaches insurrection and assassination against all those who oppose the opinion of the Anarchists.

"Notwithstanding the atrocity of the offence, this fellow's party has so far triumphed, that he and all his companions arrested under the orders of the Committee of Twelve, have been liberated from prison. The gaols are once more thrown open, and I very much fear that it is only preparatory to some general and fatal insurrection. I question whether the Executive Power has sufficient force to oppose the Anarchists.

"As soon as *Hebert*, after his release, appeared in the Hall of the Commons, a young female Citizen begged permission to crown him with a wreath of oak; but he refused the honour, and placed it on the head of the statue of *Rousseau*. This comedy ended by a decree, 'That the 28th of May should henceforth be inscribed in the Public Calendar, under the title *The Day of Friendship*'."

The rising began on May 31st. On June 2nd the armed crowd from the revolutionary sections surrounded the Convention. The assembly surrendered without bloodshed and the 'Girondin' majority leaders were placed under house arrest. Their indictment, trial and execution on the usual charges of conspiracy took place in October. France passed under the centralized revolutionary dictatorship of the Jacobins.

On July 13th, Marat was murdered in his bath by Charlotte Corday. A lonely idealist, she struck to avenge the King; she had no accomplices, but The Times *saw that the 'Girondins' would be cast as fellow-conspirators.*

July 23rd, 1793

We have been so fortunate as to obtain the PARIS Gazettes down to the 16th inst. They have reached us with greater expedition than any that have been received from Paris since the communication between Calais and Dover was interrupted. They were received on Sunday night, but unfortunately too late to be made use of for our Paper of yesterday. When we consider the nature of their contents, they are by far the most interesting of any that have been received from France for many weeks past. They announce that MARAT has been assassinated by a WOMAN, who has since confessed, that she thought she had done the best act of her life, by ridding the world of such a monster.

Hitherto, the Revolutionists of every description, whether *Constitutionalists, Republicans* or *Anarchists,* have invented plots against the loyal subjects of France, in order to render them odious to the People, and to instigate murder. Premeditated assassination has at length levelled *King* MARAT with the dust; a man, who in all the stages of the Revolution, has been used by all parties as the instrument of their crimes. The party of *la Gironde* is accused of having armed this woman to commit the murder; and this confirms an observation that has been often made by us, *that sooner or later, these wretches, glutted with the effusion of blood, would cut each other's throats, and thereby accomplish the decrees of divine justice.* But whether the *Girondists* committed this act or not, is at present immaterial; it will however, certainly serve as a pretext for bringing the heads of this party immediately to the scaffold.

July 26th, 1793

MARAT, that infamous regicide, who lately fell beneath the assassin's dagger, and who so justly merited the fate he has met with, is thus described:

He was a little man, of a cadaverous complexion, and a countenance exceedingly expressive of the bloody disposition of his mind. To a painter of massacre, he would have afforded a fine portrait for the chief murderer. His head would be inestimable for such a subject.

His eyes resembled those of the *tyger cat,* and there was a kind of ferociousness in his looks that corresponded with the savage fierceness of that animal.

The only artifice he used in favour of those lineaments of the beast, was that of wearing a round hat, so far pulled down before, as to hide a great part of his countenance.

He was an active Member of the *General Council of the Commons.* He loved carnage like a vulture, and delighted in human sacrifices.

But the uplifted arm of Divine vengeance cut him off in the midst of his career, and allowed him only the short time to say, *"I am dying."*

.   .   .

PARIS, JULY 18.

The funeral of *Marat* was celebrated the day before yesterday, with the greatest pomp and solemnity. All the Sections joined in the procession, some with their colours, but all of them with their standards. An immense crowd of people attended it. Four women bore the bathing-machine in which *Marat* was standing when he was assassinated; his shirt, stained with blood, was carried by another Amazon, at the top of a pike. After this followed a wooden bedstead, on which the corpse of *Marat* was carried by citizens. His head was uncovered, and the gash made by the knife of the assassin could be easily distinguished. The procession paraded through several streets, and was saluted on its march by several discharges of artillery. At half past ten o'clock at night the remains of *Marat* were deposited in a grave dug in the yard of the club of the Cordeliers, between four linden trees. At the base of his bed of state the following words were inscribed:

"MARAT, *the Friend of the People, assassinated by the Enemies of the People. Enemies of the Country, moderate your joy; he will find avengers."*

Charlotte la Corde was tried yesterday for the murder of the Friend of People, by the Revolutionary Tribunal. At the beginning of her trial she thus addressed her Judges:

"I did not expect to appear before you—I always thought that I should be delivered up to the rage of the people, torn in pieces, and that my head, stuck on the top of a pike, would have preceded *Marat* on his state-bed, to serve as a rallying point to Frenchmen, if there are still any worthy of that name. But,

happen what will, if I have the honours of the *guillotine,* and my
clay-cold remains are buried, they will soon have conferred upon
them the honours of the Pantheon, and my memory will be more
honoured in France than that of *Judith* in Bethulia." Sentence of
death was then pronounced upon this resolute woman, and she
was executed in the evening.

.   .   .

NATIONAL CONVENTION.

MONDAY, JULY 15,—CONCLUDED.

The Minister at War acquainted the convention with the
dismission of *Biron.*

The Convention passed a decree, containing four articles,
for completing the annihilation of every title or record of the
ancient Nobility.

Drouet complained, that the discourse he had pronounced
yesterday on the death of Marat, had not been inserted in the
Minutes. "I then announced," said he, "that, for 24 hours, the
remains of our colleague remain without burial.—*Bentabole*
demanded, that they should think of honouring his memory.

The assembly ordered Drouet's speech, the *proces-verbal* of
the death of Marat, and the declarations of Duperret, to be
inserted in the minutes.

"On the eve of the death of Marat," said *David,*[1] "the
Society of the Jacobins sent to Maure and me the news. I found
him in an attitude which struck me: he had a billet of wood near
him, on which were ink and paper; and his hand, which had just
come out of the bath, wrote his last thoughts for the safety of the
people. Yesterday the surgeon, who embalmed his body, sent to
ask in what manner it should be exposed to the view of the
people in the church of the Cordeliers. No part of his body can
be uncovered, for he had a leprosy, and his blood was totally
inflamed; but I thought it interesting to present him in the
attitude in which I found him, writing for the happiness of the
people."

[1] Jacques-Louis David not only painted scenes of the Revolution but designed
many of its pageants. He is referring to his 'Marat Assassiné'. David became
court painter to Napoleon, but at the Restoration was exiled to Brussels as a
'regicide'.

August 10th, 1793

At the procession of the interment of MARAT, among the extraordinary circumstances which attended his funeral, four women bore the bath in which he was assassinated, and placed it in the Church of the *Cordeliers*, where he was buried, multitudes came round it, and made the sign of the cross in emerging their fingers into that supposed sacred water. The women of the markets, the most severe and violent, most fervently prayed for the salvation of his aethereal spirit.

The body of Marat in eight hours after his death was so putrified and discoloured, that to expose it to the public they were obliged to paint it white, and to colour red his lips and the wound he had received, which was entirely mortified, from the state of his health before his death; he was besides exceedingly reduced and emaciated by his indefatigable attention to the service of his party.

His funeral was attended by all the Deputies of the Convention and Administrative Bodies of Paris, to the Church of the *Cordeliers*, in the same section wherein he died.

The first Committee of Public Safety was set up in April 1793. It took its final form in July, when Robespierre became one of its twelve members, and acted in effect as the executive government of France. The Committee of General Security was responsible for policing, but was overridden by the Committee of Public Safety in the contest for control of the Revolutionary Tribunal, the instrument of the terror.

Robespierre did not share the agnosticism or atheism of his colleagues. From the 'Festival of Reason' held in Notre-Dame, he developed his own 'Cult of the Supreme Being' which, at the time of his fall, was held to be a method of adding to his own dictatorship the role of pontiff of a new 'fanaticism'.

November 20th, 1793

PARIS, Nov. 12.

A grand Festival dedicated to *Reason* and *Truth* was yesterday celebrated in the *ci-devant* Cathedral of Paris. In the middle of this church was erected a mount, and on it a very plain temple, the *façade* of which bore the following inscription:—*A la Philosophie*. Before the gate of this temple were placed the busts of the most celebrated philosophers. The Torch of Truth was in the summit of the mount upon the *Altar of Reason,* spreading light. The Convention and all the constituted Authorities assisted at the ceremony.

Two rows of young girls, dressed in white, each wearing a crown of oak leaves, crossed before the Altar of Reason, at the sound of Republican music; each of the girls inclined before the torch, and ascended the summit of the mountain. Liberty then came out of the Temple of Philosophy towards a throne made of grass, to receive the homage of the Republicans of both sexes, who sung an hymn in her praise, extending their arms at the same time towards her. Liberty descended afterwards to return to the Temple, and on re-entering it, she turned about, casting a look of benevolence on her friends.—When she got in, every one expressed with enthusiasm the sensations which the goddess excited in them by songs of joy, and they swore never to cease to be faithful to her.

By the end of the year, the Jacobin dictatorship had consolidated itself. Carnot's new army had defeated the foreign enemies in the north-east. Within France, the Vendée rising had been broken and Lyon, which had been taken over by an anti-jacobin regime, was recaptured and subjected to murderous reprisals.

In the capital, however, the dictatorship of Robespierre was provoking growing opposition from the left-wing Commune of Paris. Against his wishes, the Commune closed all places of worship in Paris in November. After months of struggle, Hébert and the Cordeliers Club threatened another insurrection (the 'fourth Revolution' predicted below). They were arrested and executed on March 25th. Danton and his followers, who tried to manipulate both sides to win a more libertarian and democratic regime, went to the guillotine on April 5th.

March 24th, 1794

On Saturday we received the PARIS GAZETTES down to the 17th

105

instant, which contain the sequel of the very important news given in this Paper of that day, which seems to announce a *fourth Revolution* in PARIS within the short space of five years. The following remarks, on what is now passing, will not be found uninteresting:—

The city of Paris discovers symptoms of convulsion similar to those which preceded the two last Revolutions. A few days prior to that of the 10th of August 1792, La FAYETTE made a solemn renunciation of the Jacobins: he was supported by the majority of the Legislative Assembly; but the Jacobins, forming an union with the *Commune* of Paris, soon triumphed over *La Fayette,* the *Feuillans,* and the *Royalists.* The Revolution of the 31st of May was preceded by the denunciation of the Anarchists, and the imprisonment of *Hebert,* Procurator of the *Commune.* In a short time, however, the Anarchists and the Commune subjected the Brissotines to the very same fate the latter had before brought on the *Feuillans* and the *Royalists.*

Since that period, the ANARCHISTS, known under the title of the *Mountaineers,* have split into two factions; that of the Committee of Public Safety, at the head of which is *Robespierre;* and that of the *Commune of Paris,* of which *Hebert* is the principal agent. *Robespierre* has under his influence the Executive Council, the Committees of the Convention, and a part of the Jacobins. *Hebert* is supported by the Cordeliers, by a part of the Jacobins under the guidance of *Collot d'Herbois,* and by the *Commune.*

For a long time have the two parties attacked each other with a considerable degree of violence, but not, however, without blending some discretion with their anger. Latterly indeed, *Hebert* has displayed less caution, by making direct attacks on *Robespierre,* and by distributing placards, calculated to produce an insurrection fatal to his adversaries. His apparent motive was to force the Convention to try *Chabot, Bazire,* and several other Deputies, accused of having received money from foreign Powers to bring about a conspiracy. *Robespierre,* now become moderate, and feeling a desire to stop the violent movements of those who wished to step even beyond the Revolution, has employed all his address to delay the trial of his old friends.

The intrigues of the *Cordeliers* and the *Commune,* threatening to shake the power of the Committee of Public Safety, the latter has caused the authors of these intrigues to be apprehended. As this apprehension, however, has produced very alarming commotions in Paris, the partizans of *Hebert* and his companions, taking care to influence the public with an idea that they are the unhappy victims of their own zeal and patriotism, *Robespierre*, to appease the commotions among the people, has found himself at length reduced to the necessity of prevailing on the Convention to hasten the trials of *Chabot* and the other Deputies, to the end that an accusation might not be brought against him of affording shelter to the enemies of the Republic.

What will be the result of all these commotions? The very great influence of *Robespierre* seems to promise him a complete triumph; but we have found by experience, that the *Commune of Paris* has invariably obtained victory, at the very moment when it was thought to have been subdued. We know also, that in the sequel, the minority has constantly effected the destruction of the majority; and that the most violent of the Anarchists have always got the better of those of a more moderate cast. We therefore deem it prudent to suspend our opinion until we are possessed of further facts. This, however, is certain—either that *Robespierre* and his Committee will be massacred, or that the heads of *Hebert* and his accomplices will be carried to the block. But whatever party may get the better, the Republic will still be subjected to an anarchy more or less atrocious in its nature; and what is now passing only lays the foundation for a new *Septemberizing.*

All the Sections are on foot to demand the death of the rich, as being the essential enemies of the Republic; the prisons are more and more crouded; *St. Just* has demanded and obtained the formation of six Popular Tribunals, similar to those which resided at the atrocious deeds of September 1792, in order to *clear the prisons.*

By a last Revolutionary Act, it is proposed to give a new energy to the people, and to prepare for the execution of 61 Members of the Convention, accused of entertaining the principles of *Brissotinism.*

April 8th, 1794

By the FLANDERS MAIL of yesterday, we received the PARIS Gazettes of the 1st instant, which contain news of the utmost importance; no less than the arrest of DANTON, LACROIX, CAMILLE DESMOULINS, and PHILIPPEAUX, and Members of the Convention. Here is again another instance of ROBESPIERRE'S growing power! There is every appearance of its being this man's intention to get himself declared DICTATOR.

We have not, at present, time to make all the observations that naturally occur to us on hearing this news, or on reading BARRERE'S speech in this day's paper.

When the late reconciliation took place between ROBESPIERRE and DANTON, we remarked, that it proceeded rather from the fear which these two famous Revolutionists entertained of each other, than from mutual affection;—we added, that it would last only till the more dexterous of the two should, find an opportunity to destroy his rival. The time, fatal to DANTON, is at length arrived: He falls with the *Cordeliers,* of whom, originally, he was the firmest support; and we make no doubt but that if MARAT, who was his agent, and directed his convulsive motions, were alive at this moment, he would partake in the disgrace of his friend. Perhaps, in the day when DANTON, shall act his last part upon the scaffold, MARAT will be dragged from the *Pantheon,* to be trailed in the dirt, which ought to have been his fate long since.

We do not comprehend the reason why CAMILLE DESMOULINS, who was so openly protected by ROBESPIERRE, is crushed in the triumph of this Dictator; or why PHILIPPEAUX, the denouncer of RONSIN, is on the eve of suffering the same fate as his enemy. But these, and many more mysteries must soon be unveiled: every day produces some new event to excite our surprise; and it is not the least remarkable circumstance, that BARRERE should pronounce the new Government to be determined to support RELIGION and VIRTUE!!!

The Society for Constitutional Information, founded in 1780 but now revived under the influence of Horne Tooke, was one of the network of revolutionary groups which looked to France. The London Corresponding Society, set up in 1792, has been described as the first political association of workers in recorded history. A series of repressive laws was passed, and 'corresponding societies' were finally banned in 1796.

May 5th, 1794

The *Horne* of sedition is blowing up a flame that most probably will consume itself. The notes it sounded at the Crown and Anchor last Friday, must reach the ears of justice.

The *Society for Constitutional Information* held a Meeting at the Crown and Anchor, in the Strand, on Friday last, where toasts of the most seditious tendency were drank, and sentiments expressed which ought to send the speakers to Botany Bay. Were the *feeble abilities* of these men equal to their *strong inclinations,* they would subvert our Constitution, and destroy every atom of public and private property.

The number of seditionists who met on the above occasion, amounted to 300 persons; among whom were not to be found above three who possessed an acre of land in this country. They were men mostly in desperate circumstances, who had every thing to gain and nothing to lose, by a Revolution. They toasted success to the French, sung *the Marseillois treasonable Hymn,* and *ça ira*, arraigned the justice of the law that had punished traitors in Scotland, Ireland, and England, and gave the health of those traitors. They abused and vilified the House of Commons, called the Royal Family and the Nobility of Great Britain, beggars; said it was the interest of the people to join with those struggling in the cause against which our Country was fighting. In short they did every thing short of *active rebellion.*

The British army played a small and generally unsuccessful part in the first years of war. It was the Navy which provided the first unqualified victory, the 'Glorious First of June'.

June 11th, 1794

IMPORTANT NAVAL VICTORY ! ! ! !

Yesterday evening, about eight o'clock, Sir ROGER CURTIS, First Captain of Lord HOWE's Fleet, arrived at the Admiralty with dispatches of the greatest importance. They state, that on the first of June, Lord HOWE fell in with the French Fleet, when an engagement commenced; and after a severe conflict of many hours, with as severe fighting as ever was known, victory was declared in favour of the English, by the capture of SIX SAIL OF THE LINE, and TWO SUNK.

Both fleets have suffered considerably, Sir ROGER CURTIS reports, that the French fought with great bravery. Most of the enemy's ships were mauled in their hulls, and tried to escape without waiting for each other.

We are sorry to state the death of Capt. JAMES MONTAGU, who was killed early in the action. Admiral PASLEY has lost a leg, and so has Admiral BOWYER.

The slaughter was immense on board the French Fleet; and we are sorry also to add, we have lost a great many seamen, to the number, in some ships, of 60 or 70 men killed and wounded.

Sir ROGER CURTIS landed at Falmouth on the 7th, and on his way to town was unfortunately overturned in a chaise, and bruised his arm a good deal; so much so that he has it in a sling.

We hope that Admiral MONTAGUE's squadron which sailed on the arrival of the *Audacious,* Capt. Parker, the other day from Plymouth, will fall in with and pick up some of the enemy's straggling ships.

June 16th, 1794

NATIONAL CONVENTION

SITTING OF MAY 26 CONTINUED.

Continuation of BARRERE's speech on the DECREE to *give no quarter to the British and Hanoverian soldiers.*

Barrere next proceeded to advert to the time of *Hebert* and *Danton,* when a correspondence was established between Paris and London, to keep up a constant circulation of atrocious calumnies, and of plots tending to cut off certain members of the Convention. He expatiated on the rumours circulated in the English papers, respecting the pretended assassination of the Committees of Public and General Safety; and on the plan of a Dictatorship, which the Ministers of GEORGE ascribed to ROBESPIERRE, with a view of rendering him odious. He complained, as an especial grievance, that in the English journals, the troops of the Republic were stiled *the soldiers of Robespierre,* the French armies entitled *Conventional gangs of robbers and cut-throats,* and a despotism injurious to the National Representation ascribed to the Committee of Public Safety.

"Thus, continued *Barrere,* have the English constantly aimed at bewildering the public opinion. At the first period of the Revolution, they insinuated, that we fought for a change of government alone. At the second, they endeavoured to instil a belief, that there was in France a secret plan of Dictatorship, which they ascribed to the Committee, to transfer it afterwards to *Robespierre.* Calumnies such as these are more stupid than atrocious: they are only calculated to amuse the English in their pot-houses, and may be considered as a phantom, which they whirl at will over the heads of the incorruptible Republicans, whose fertile labours, seconded by the courage of the armies and the might of the people, will one day annihilate England. Kings, to expose us to hatred, are obliged to make us resemble them, and to speak of "the troops of a Deputy," as the troops of GEORGE are spoken of. British speculators! dealers in treasons and slaves! bankers in crimes! we abhor you! The hatred of Rome against Carthage is revived in the souls of Frenchmen, as is the *Punic* faith in the hearts of the English."

Barrere next accused the English Government of having purchased corn in France, not for consumption, but to leave it to rot and decay; of having intercepted the corn by sea, to starve the French; of having corrupted the human species; of having destroyed one part of mankind to enslave the other; of having formed the best concerted plan to organize murder; and of having put in execution a regular plan of famine.

"The English, added he, cannot belie their origin. Descendants of the Carthaginians, they sold bulls-hides and slaves. Caesar, when he landed on Great Britain, found in it a ferocious people, disputing with the wolves the right of the forests. Its successive civilization, its civil and maritime wars, every thing bears the stamp of its ferocity. In Bengal, this nation famished several millions of men to subjugate a small number, and in America and at the Antilles it encouraged the slave trade. In North America it ravaged the coast, destroyed the ports, burned the towns, and massacred the inhabitants of the plains. It forced the American prisoners to become the hangmen of their brethren; and corrupted the humanity of the savages, by offering a reward for the scalp of every white which should be brought to the English Commandant."

June 20th, 1794

A grand festival was yesterday celebrated here, dedicated to the SUPREME BEING.

Precisely at five in the morning, a general summons was made throughout Paris.

By this summons, all male and female Citizens were invited instantly to decorate their houses with the cherished colours of Liberty, either by displaying new flags, or embellishing their old ones with garlands of flowers and greens. They then repaired to the principal rendezvous of their respective Sections, there to wait the signal for setting out.

The men were all without arms, if we except the youths of from 14 to 18 years of age, who were provided, either with swords and fusils, or with pikes.

In each Section these youths formed a square battalion, marching 12 in front; and in the midst of them were placed the streamers and flag of the armed force of the Section, carried by those to whom they were usually entrusted.

Each adult Citizen and each youth held in his hand an oak branch; while the matrons and young girls, arrayed in the colours of Liberty, held in theirs, the former, bouquets of roses, and the latter baskets of flowers.

To occupy the *Mountain,* elevated in the field of *La Re-Union,* each Section selected 10 old men; 10 matrons; 10 young girls, their age between 15 and 20 years; 10 youths, their age between 15 and 18 years; and 10 male infants, their age below eight years. The ten matrons, selected by each Section, were clad in white, and carried a scarf of tri-coloured ribbon, extending to the left side from the right shoulder. The ten young girls were also in white, and with similar scarfs: their hair was interwoven with flowers. The ten youths were armed with sabres. . . . .

When the procession reached the National Garden, a deputation announced to the Convention that every preparation was made to celebrate the festival of the Divinity.

The Convention, preceded by large bands of music, then repaired to the Pavilion of Unity, and placed themselves on a superb Amphitheatre, when the President ascended the Tribunal, and displayed to the people the motives of this solemn festival, inviting them to honour the great Author of Nature. During the perfomance of a symphony, the President, armed with the *Torch of Truth*, descended from the Amphitheatre, and approached a monument, erected in a circular bason of stone, representing the Monster of Atheism. From this monument, set fire to by the President, Wisdom sprang up.

By each Section a Commissioner was appointed, to lead to the spot fixed on for that purpose, the 50 persons selected by the Section to be stationed on the Mountain; and to each of them, as well as to the Commissioner, was delivered a card, which was worn in a conspicuous way.

All the inhabitants of Paris were provided with branches of oak, bouquets, garlands and baskets of flowers, and were ornamented with the colours of Liberty.

Precisely at eight in the morning, a discharge of artillery from the Pont Neuf, announced the arrival of the moment for repairing to the National Garden. The inhabitants of each Section now repaired thither in two columns. . . . .

The President again addressed the people; and at this moment a second beat of drums announced the departure for the field of *La Re-Union*.

Order of THE MARCH thither:

A detachment of cavalry, preceded by trumpets; corps of sappers and pumpers; gunners; an hundred drums, and the pupils of the military academy; 24 Sections: the group of old men, &c. before described; bands of music; the National Convention encircled by a tri-coloured ribbon, carried by infancy adorned with violets, by youth adorned with myrtle, by virility adorned with oak, and by old age adorned with the leaves of the vine and olive. Each Representative carried in his hand a bouquet of ears of corn, flowers, and fruits; and in the centre was a car with a trophy, representing the arts, trades and productions of the French territory, and drawn by eight heifers ornamented with festoons and garlands. Next came an hundred drums; 24 Sections, in the same order with the preceding ones, with a car filled with blind children, who sang during the way a hymn to the Divinity; and lastly, a body of cavalry.

When arrived at the field of *La Re-Union*, the musicians performed a hymn to the Supreme Being, and afterwards a grand symphony. Several airs composed for the occasion were sung, and a general discharge of artillery made amidst the shouts of *"Vive la Republique"*.

This concluded the ceremony; and the procession returned to Paris.

In Paris, Robespierre's position continued to decay. The population, though deprived of its radical leaders, was enraged at a relaxation of the price controls reluctantly introduced the previous year. The 'Law of 22 Prairial' (10th June), denying prisoners before the Tribunal the right to a defender, accelerated the terror and angered the Committee of Public Security, which considered that it had been flouted. Robespierre's hold on the Convention weakened; personal quarrels divided the Committee of Public Safety. On July 26th, Robespierre defended his policies before the Convention and argued that a fresh group of public enemies — whom he did not name — must be eliminated. Common fear united his opponents, and he was arrested the following day with Saint-Just, his most loyal supporter. The Commune attempted to defend him, but forces of the Convention broke into the Hôtel de Ville and seized him and his colleagues on the morning of 10th Thermidor (July 28th). They were executed a few hours later.

The first Times *report of Thermidor was totally garbled. A better version was put together at Printing House Square over the weekend.*

August 16th, 1794

Since the early part of the month of June, when ROBESPIERRE forced the Convention to revoke the Decree of Adjournment, which a great majority had just then carried, upon the question of the *Organization of a Revolutionary Tribunal,* two parties declared themselves in its bosom; and when TALLIEN survived the accusation of being a villain, a conspirator, and an *Hebertist,* which were made against him by Robespierre, it became a matter of doubt which faction would be victorious.

We have followed the various pursuits of both; the perpetual declamations of the Dictator at the Jacobins—the small effect produced by his presence and speeches; and we have informed the Public of the decline of his influence, and the dangers which threatened his party and person. We have repeatedly called the attention of our readers to all these events, and to predict the approaching catastrophe with which the ruling faction was menaced.

114

Time has realized these events:—Either ROBESPIERRE and his adherents must fall, or the MAJORITY of the CONVENTION pass under the edge of the *guillotine.*

ROBESPIERRE'S greatest enemies were in the very bosom of the Committee of Public Safety. The first blows were struck by BARRERE and ST. JUST. On the 27th of July, BARRERE mounted the Tribune in the Convention, and denounced the DICTATOR, whose mouth-piece and apologist he had been for the last six months. Several Members threw themselves upon ROBESPIERRE, and murdered him with poniards, crying out, *"Perish the Tyrant!"* The two Factions fought in the Hall, and their mutual fury reached the city, where the conflict is said to have lasted three days, in which time from 10 to 14,000 men fell. Among the Deputies killed are mentioned ROBESPIERRE, *junior,* the Dictator's brother, COUTHON, LAVALETTE, DAMAS, and ST. JUST. The latter was killed fighting in the streets, at the head of the *Anti-Robespierrian* Party. *Barrere* was soon after proclaimed President of the Convention.

August 18th, 1794

FRANCE

EXECUTION OF ROBESPIERRE AND HIS PARTY.

Three factions have successively reigned in France since ROYALTY was abolished:—That of the *Girondins,* that of the *Hebertists,* and lastly that of ROBESPIERRE. Their Chiefs have each in their turn fallen a sacrifice; and it is not difficult to discover, that the faction which has just obtained the sceptre of anarchy, will soon experience the same fate.

Of all the Chiefs of the different factions which have successively reigned in the volcano of the French Revolution, ROBESPIERRE was the man whose Government promised to be the most durable; because he had the character of being the most incorruptible, and of being the man who had shewn the least variation in his conduct. The cause of his overthrow will, no doubt, be accounted for in the number of terrible executions which he ordered, and which brought upon him an host of enemies. But how is it possible to be harsh and not sanguinary, in aspiring to become the Leader of a Revolutionary Government, which can only exist amidst storms and factions?

We shall not, however, now anticipate the consequences of this new Revolution. The circumstances are not yet sufficiently known to comment on them. We have therefore confined ourselves in giving a very faithful analysis of the proceedings of the Convention, from the 27th of July to the 30th, during which time the Sittings were PERMANENT day and night. Our extracts have been made with great care; and we trust the history will be found clear and connected. It is taken from the Papers of the *Moniteur* of the 26th, 27th, 28th, 29th, 30th, and 31st of July; and we believe there are not three copies of so late a date in town.

In the night of the 27th and 28th, a seditious assemblage of ROBESPIERRE's adherents invested the COMMITTEE of GENERAL SAFETY, broke open the doors of it, and forcibly took possession of several pretended conspirators who were there under arrest, whom they conducted to the house of the *Commune*, where the Council General had raised the standard of rebellion, and had ordered the Sections of the city to communicate only with them, and to arm against the Convention. The Council General had moreover ordered that all officers and commandants nominated by the Legislative Body, should be arrested.

The CONVENTION, on being informed of these facts, decreed, that all who should oppose its will, should be placed out of the reach of the law. It chose 12 of its Members to go to the National guard-house, and discharge the functions of the Representatives of the People, in the same manner as was done at the armies.—"Go, (said the Convention to these 12 Members), and may the sun not rise, until the rebels and conspirators are placed within the reach of the national justice."

By three o'clock on the morning of the 28th, the Representatives had got possession of the house of the *Commune*, with all the traitors who had shut themselves up in it. In the house was found a seal, very newly engraved, with the emblem of the *Fleur de Lys*. About the same hour, the Department of Paris presented an Address to the Convention, congratulating it on the steps it had taken for unmasking plots and traitors, and for once more saving the country from the brink of destruction; and it assured the Convention of its full co-operation in annihilating all seditious men. This deputation was followed by others from the different Sections, who assured the Convention that it would always find them ready to rally around it.

In the same sitting were arrested, *Vivier*, President of the Jacobins; *Taschereau*, a confidant of *Robespierre's; St. Just; Le Bas; Payan*, the National agent; *Henriot*, the Commandant of the National Guard, who afterwards threw himself from a window and was killed; *Fleurio*, Mayor of Paris; *Sijas; La Valette; Boulanger; Daubini; Dumas*, President of the Revolutionary Tribunal; *Nicolas*, one of the Jury of the same Tribunal, and several others whose names are not mentioned. *Le Bas* shot himself by a pistol; the two *Robespierres* and *Couthon* attempted to do the same but only wounded themselves; and were then taken into custody, to undergo the punishment of the law in a more public manner.

On the 28th, at ten o'clock at night, the above persons and many others were executed by torchlight in the *Place de la Revolution*, amidst an immense body of people (as many as were present at the late KING's execution), who rent the air with the shouts of *Vive la Republique! Vive la Convention!*

There are various reports of subsequent massacres to those of the 28th and 29th ult. They may be true; but certainly there is no regular account in town of a later date than is in our possession. We have therefore contented ourselves with inserting that only which we know to be the fact.

Billaud Varennes, Barrere, and *Collot d'Herbois,* foreseeing the downfall of ROBESPIERRE's party, had the address to join the predominating faction; and thus have saved their necks.

Thermidor marked the end of the Revolution's five years of accelerating radicalism. Within a year, moderates were in control and the 'bourgeois republic' was embarked on the slow drift towards the coup of 19 Brumaire (November 10th, 1799). On that day, full authority passed to three Consuls, of whom the youngest was General Bonaparte.

FURTHER READING

History of The Times, 1785-1841, London, 1935

Briggs, Asa, *The Age of Improvement,* London, 1959
Burke, E., *Reflections on the Revolution in France,* London, 1910, and many other editions
Cobban, A. (ed.), *The Debate on the French Revolution,* London, 1950
George, Dorothy, English Political Caricature, vols 1 and 2, Oxford, 1959
Lefebvre, G., *La Révolution française,* London, 1962
Paine, Thomas, *Complete Writings,* New York, 1934
Rudé, George, *The Crowd in the French Revolution,* Oxford, 1959
Rudé, George, *Revolutionary Europe 1783-1815,* London, 1964
Soboul, Albert, *The Parisians Sans-Culottes and the French Revolution 1793-4,* Oxford, 1964
Sydenham, M.J., *The Girondins,* London, 1961
Thompson, J.M., *The French Revolution,* Oxford, 1959
Young, Arthur, *Travels in France* (ed. Constantia Maxwell), Cambridge, 1929